insight text guide

Mark Eckersley

No Sugar

Jack Davis

First published in 2013. Reprinted with corrections in 2014, 2015 (twice), 2016, 2018, 2019, 2020, 2021, 2025.

Insight Publications Pty Ltd
3/350 Charman Road
Cheltenham VIC 3192
Australia
Tel: +61 3 8571 4950
Email: books@insightpublications.com.au

www.insightpublications.com.au

National Library of Australia Cataloguing-in-Publication entry:

Eckersley, Mark, author.
Jack Davis' No sugar / Mark Eckersley.
9781922243171 (paperback)
Insight text guide.
Includes bibliographical references.
For secondary school age.
Davis, Jack, 1917–2000. No sugar.
Davis, Jack, 1917–2000.—Criticism and interpretation.
A822.3

Other ISBNs:
9781925175165 (digital)

Cover design: Modern Art Production Group

Printed by Markono Print Media Pte Ltd

contents

CHARACTER MAP

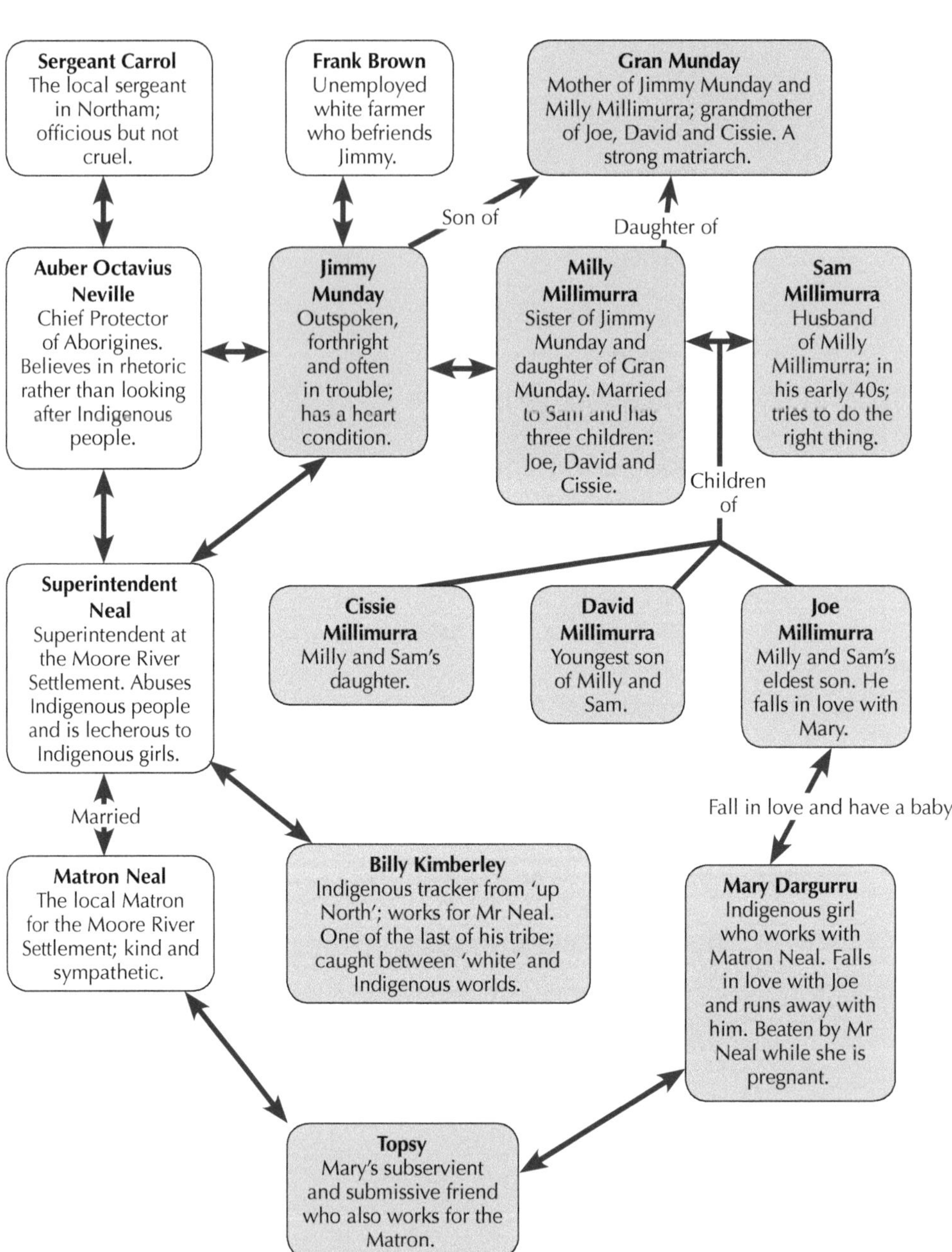

OVERVIEW

About the playwright

Jack Davis was an Indigenous Australian playwright and poet, who was born on 11 March 1917. He was a descendant of the Nyoongah and was raised at Yarloop and the Moore River Native Settlement.

When his father died, Jack Davis left school and moved to the North West of Western Australia to work as a labourer, boundary rider and drover. Largely self-educated, Davis furthered his education by writing after long hard working days. He wrote down observations, stories and poems about his experiences and the struggles of his people.

Davis was involved in advocacy and the Aboriginal Advancement Council in the lead-up to the 1967 Referendum which gave the Australian Federal Government control of Indigenous Australians. It also acknowledged Indigenous peoples as being counted in the Census and having the same rights as other Australians. With the success of the Referendum, new horizons opened up for many Indigenous people. In 1967, Davis became Director of the Aboriginal Centre in Perth where he promoted Indigenous Australian cultures while writing articles, poetry and stories. His first book, an anthology of poetry called *The First Born*, was published in 1970. Davis became the first chairman of the Aboriginal Lands Trust of Western Australia in 1971, championing Indigenous causes. He mentored the work of Australian Indigenous writers in *Identity*, a quarterly journal he published as Managing Editor of the Aboriginal Publications Foundation.

As early as 1972, Davis saw drama as a natural medium to promote modern Indigenous stories. His first play, *The Steel and the Stone*, was a semi-autobiographical dramatic piece exploring the history of the Moore River Native Settlement. It had a week's run at the Bunbury Arts Festival in 1972. Davis wrote another short play in 1975 called *The Biter Bit*, which is about a group of country Indigenous people who go to Sydney and con a con man.

In 1976, Davis was made an MBE (Member of the British Empire) for services to Indigenous Australians and in the same year he developed the script for *Kullark*, an Indigenous drama about the first contact between 'whites and blacks'. Director Andrew Ross included the play in the National Theatre Company of Western Australia Theatre-in-Education program, giving young Indigenous actor Ernie Dingo his first major role. In 1978, Davis published another collection of poems entitled *Jagardoo: Poems from Aboriginal Australia*.

Davis then began writing *The Dreamers* with the Swan River Stage Company which premiered at Perth's Dolphin Theatre in 1982 as part of the Festival of Perth. In 1983, the National Theatre Company of Western Australia and the Australian Elizabethan Theatre Trust mounted a four-month national tour.

The death of sixteen-year old Indigenous youth John Pat in police custody in 1983 led to Davis writing the moving poem 'John Pat' (published in the 1988 poetry anthology *John Pat and Other Poems*). Davis became a strong lifelong advocate for the work of the Deaths in Custody Watch Committee.

The plays *Honey Spot* (a children's play which looks at cultural and environmental understanding) and *No Sugar* were written in 1985. *No Sugar* premiered at the Festival of Perth and was chosen to go overseas to the World Theatre Festival in Vancouver, Canada, in 1986. In that year Davis became a co-winner of the Australian Writers' Guild Award for Best Stage Play for *No Sugar* and was made a Member of the Order of Australia (AM). Together, *The Dreamers, No Sugar* and *Barungin* (1989) form the *First Born Trilogy*.

Davis' other plays include *Moorli and the Leprechauns, Barungin* (*Smell the Wind*), *Death of a Tree, In Our Town* (1990) and the incomplete play *Triangle* (written with his wife Madelon). During the 1990s Davis continued to be an inspiration for Indigenous Australian writers, performers and activists. After a long battle with sickness, he died in his sleep on 17 March 2000 at the age of eighty-three.

Synopsis

The Millimurra-Munday family live in poverty in a run-down camp at the Government Well Aboriginal Reserve outside Northam, Western Australia in 1929. Government rations are being steadily reduced. In Perth, A. O. Neville (the Chief Protector of Aborigines) decides to further cut rations to the 'natives' while planning to move them away from Government Well.

Frank, an unemployed white farmer, befriends Jimmy Munday and comes for dinner. Frank gives alcohol to Jimmy and his brother-in-law Sam Millimurra – though this is illegal. The next morning, Frank is charged with supplying alcohol to natives and is sentenced to six weeks imprisonment, Jimmy is given three months and Sam is fined.

Soon after, Sergeant Carrol is instructed to move all the natives from Government Well to the Moore River Settlement supposedly because of a scabies outbreak, but the real reasons are political. After some resistance the families leave Northam and arrive at the Moore River Settlement where they are under the charge of Superintendent Neal. Soon, young Joe (Sam's son) meets Mary Dargurru, a minor without family. They fall in love.

After hearing that Mr Neal wants to move Mary to a position at the hospital – where he has a reputation for molesting the girls in his care – Joe decides to run away with Mary back to Northam. Mr Neal finds out about this, and sends Billy the Tracker after them. Billy discovers them waiting by the train tracks, but Joe overcomes Billy and handcuffs him, and they escape.

Arriving at Northam, Joe and Mary find the camp has been destroyed. They forge a living for themselves until the Sergeant arrests Joe, sending him to gaol, and sends Mary (now pregnant) back to Moore River.

Mary refuses to follow Neal's orders to work in the hospital and swears at Neal. He beats the pregnant Mary with a whip and she escapes to Joe's family where she stays to have Gran deliver the baby.

At the 1934 Moore River Settlement Australia Day celebrations, speakers are heckled and a hymn is mocked by the Indigenous people.

Jimmy stands up and outlines all the hypocrisies of Mr Neville and the treatment of Indigenous people. He then suffers a heart attack and dies. Later, Gran delivers Mary's baby boy and when Joe arrives back from gaol, he decides to name the boy Jimmy after his uncle. Neal allows Joe and Mary to leave Moore River, making Joe sign an assurance that he won't return to Northam. Joe signs but when he, Mary and baby Jimmy are leaving, he expresses his intention to return to Northam. They start their homeland journey with the sound of a magpie squawking and Gran singing a song of farewell.

Character summaries

Jimmy (James) Munday

Jimmy is an Indigenous man of Nyoongah descent and is the main character. He is in his forties and has a heart condition. He is forthright, outspoken and angry at the treatment of his own people. He is often in trouble.

Gran Munday

Gran is the mother of Jimmy Munday and Milly Millimurra, and grandmother of Joe, David and Cissie. About sixty, she is a strong matriarchal figure with traditional knowledge and is proud of achievements such as delivering many babies in her family.

Milly Millimurra

In her late thirties, Milly is the sister of Jimmy Munday and daughter of Gran Munday. She is married to Sam Millimurra and they have three children: Joe, David and Cissie. She has a strong sense of equality yet feels that she cannot ultimately change anything.

Sam Millimurra

Sam is the husband of Milly Millimurra. He is in his early forties and is caught breaking the law with Jimmy. Unlike Jimmy, Sam is not outspoken.

Joe Millimurra

Joe is Milly and Sam's eldest son. He is in his late teens and can read. He falls in love with Mary and learns to speak up for himself and resist authority.

Cissie (Cecilia) Millimurra

Milly and Sam's daughter Cissie is in her early teens. She is a helpful girl at home and attends school.

David Millimurra

David is the youngest son of Milly and Sam; he is around eleven years old.

Mary Dargurru

Mary is an Indigenous girl of about sixteen from the Kimberley, who works with Matron Neal. She falls in love with Joe, learns to stand up for herself and has a baby with Joe.

Topsy

Topsy is Mary's subservient and submissive friend who also works for the Matron.

Billy Kimberley

An Indigenous tracker in his twenties from 'up North' who works for Mr Neal, Billy is one of the last of his tribe. He is caught between the 'white' and Indigenous worlds.

Auber Octavius Neville

Neville is the Chief Protector of Aborigines. He is in his fifties, has an office in Perth and believes in rhetoric (making speeches) rather than looking after Indigenous people.

Sergeant Carrol

The local sergeant in Northam, Carrol is in his forties. He is officious but not cruel.

Frank

Frank is an out-of-work farmer in his forties who befriends Jimmy and is put in gaol for giving him alcohol.

Superintendent Neal

Mr Neal is in his forties. Superintendent at the Moore River Settlement, he is an unsavoury character who sometimes drinks too much, and is known for his cruelty and lecherousness towards young Indigenous girls.

Matron Neal

Matron Neal is married to Superintendent Neal. The local Matron for the Moore River Settlement, she is in her forties and is kind and sympathetic.

Sister Eileen

Sister Eileen is a missionary nun at the Sunday School at Moore River Settlement. In her thirties, she is religious but believes in education rather than punishment.

BACKGROUND & CONTEXT

Historical context

No Sugar is set during the Great Depression between 1929 and 1934, a period for Indigenous Australians dominated by Protectionism/Control Policy. It explores the themes of injustice and violence, racism, Indigenous identity, dispossession, poverty, family and the impact of government controls on Australian Indigenous peoples.

Starting in 1929, at the Government Well Aboriginal Reserve outside Northam, Western Australia, the play moves on to the Moore River Native Settlement to which the Millimurra-Munday family are forcibly relocated. Northam is ninety-seven kilometres north-east of Perth, and the Government Well Aboriginal Reserve did actually exist. Forced resettlement of Indigenous Australians occurred during a number of periods of Indigenous Australian history and development.

About 40,000 to 80,000 years ago, Indigenous Australians arrived in Australia and the surrounding islands. Much of the spirituality, philosophy, cosmology, history and knowledge of Indigenous Australians' culture is contained or embedded in a notion called *alcheringa* or the 'Dreamtime'. In Australian Indigenous cultures everything leaves its mark on the land and the land is central to learning how to live one's life.

Although there are many ways to view Indigenous Australian history, one way is to see it in terms of eight chronological periods. This raises larger questions of culture, history and types of engagement between Indigenous and non-Indigenous Australians. These periods can be categorised, in chronological order, as:

- Indigenous Australian Ancient History
- Early Contact History (contact with Chinese and Dutch, trade with Macassans)
- Invasion and Wars
- Genocide

- Protectionism and Control Policy Period
- Assimilation Policy and the height of the Stolen Generation Period
- Integration and Self-Determination
- The Path to Reconciliation – Native Title, Land Rights and Apologies.

On 26 January 1788, the First Fleet under the command of Captain Arthur Phillip landed in Australia and a colony was set up in Port Jackson. The immediate effect was the decimation of many Indigenous communities due to European diseases such as smallpox, measles and tuberculosis. Australian Aboriginal and Torres Strait Islander numbers are estimated to have been between 500,000 and one million people in 1788 but had dropped to about 125,000 by 1850.

By the 1880s, the period of Control and 'Protection' policies had been instituted across most Australian colonies. Most aspects of the lives of Indigenous Australians were controlled by Aboriginal Protection Boards and some colonial governments even began to sell off parts of Aboriginal reserves. This was combined with the amended *Acts to Provide for the Protection and Management of the Aboriginal Natives* which allowed the forced removal of 'half-caste' Indigenous Australians. The granting of pastoral leases expanded particularly in Queensland and Western Australia, which led to the expansion of the powers of Aboriginal Protection Boards. The passage of the Aboriginal Act in 1905 meant that practices of forced confinement, assimilation and removal of children became endorsed as government policy.

The retelling of the history of the Swan River Settlement and Captain Stirling's declaration in Act Three, Scene Five (pp.80–1) of the play is meant to be ironic in *No Sugar*'s dramatic context. It serves as a potent reminder of the promises made and broken to the Aboriginal and Torres Strait Islander peoples.

Indigenous resistance to dispossession never stopped. In the Kimberley in Western Australia, the elder Jandamarra (the man whose life story is so dramatically told in Steve Hawke's work *Jandamarra*, produced by both Black Swan State Theatre Company and Bunuba Films) led resistance from 1894 until he was shot and killed in 1897. Resistance was met with extreme violence. The account of the Oombulgarri Massacre in 1926 where at least eleven people were killed, as told by Billy Kimberley in Act Two, Scene Six (pp.61–3), is a potent reminder of this. Many Indigenous people from the north of Western Australia dispersed or travelled in search of work with white pastoralists, the police force and institutions.

The onset of the Great Depression meant that rations were cut to Indigenous communities, and many people were moved onto less fertile reserves such as the Moore River Native Settlement established in 1918. Initially built for eighty occupants, the Moore River Settlement steadily grew until almost five hundred people lived there. Overcrowding, poor sanitation and health problems became the main hallmark of the settlement.

No Sugar can be considered to be a social realist piece of drama. Jack Davis used his own recollections and the rich oral histories he had heard about the Moore River Settlement, and combined this with some real passages from the books and speeches of Auber Octavius Neville (the real Chief Protector of Aborigines in Western Australia from 1915 until 1936). Neville was never punished or reprimanded but was given greater powers and promoted to the Commissioner of Native Affairs, a post he held until his eventual retirement in 1940.

Author's historical context

Jack Davis grew up in Yarloop and the Moore River Native Settlement. He was a descendant of the Nyoongah people of this area. His father worked initially at the Yarloop timber mill but then when Jack was about twelve, the family and many others were moved to the infamous Moore River Native Settlement. Davis started to write poetry about the poverty and violence he saw his people subjected to. He also started to learn the Nyoongah language, a language which Davis has the Munday-Millimurra family use at dramatic points in the play.

From a young age, Davis was able to read, through a combination of the mission school system alluded to in the play and having at least one adult in the family who could read. This makes the opening scene of the play, where the *Western Mail* is read aloud by Joe, a potent and realistic sequence.

Davis moved around the state, following labour-intensive jobs such as stock work and droving. He kept up his reading during these almost twenty-five years on the road. He was passionate from an early age about the rights of Indigenous peoples and in the mid-1960s he became one of many grassroots Indigenous campaigners who helped to make the 1967 National Referendum the most successful referendum in the history of Australian government. The 1967 Referendum gave the Federal Parliament constitutional care of all Indigenous people over any previous State controls. It became a strong and potent symbol of the political and moral status and rights of Indigenous people.

It was not until Jack Davis was in his fifties that he published his first anthology of poems. His work as an activist and spokesperson for Indigenous communities, along with his work editing *Identity* magazine, led him to writing more extensively on a range of issues. Davis also started to become more committed during this period to the possibilities of theatre as a medium:

> Theatre offered an opportunity to use all the talents of speech and body movement present in Aboriginal oral literature and dance since time began. It was an exciting way of reaching a wide audience. I started writing a play called *The Steel and the Stone*. (Davis in Cheeson 1988, p.55)

The Steel and the Stone came under the eyes of Andrew Ross, who was the Youth Director of the National Theatre Company. A lifelong artistic partnership between Ross and Davis was formed. Ross encouraged Davis to write a longer and more dramatically complex version of *The Steel and the Stone* which became *The Dreamers*. *The Dreamers* finally premiered in 1982 at the Festival of Perth with the Swan River Stage Company under the direction of Andrew Ross. The production then toured nationally with a cast that included Jack Davis, Ernie Dingo, Lynnette and Maxine Narkle, John Pell and others.

At this point it is useful to address the different concepts of authenticity, ownership and models of collaboration evident in Australian Indigenous work like that of Davis. From a Western or non-Indigenous perspective, Davis' insistence on using some of his relatives and some untrained actors who had 'lived the life portrayed' in his plays (Casey 2004, p.153) might be considered strange, but from an Indigenous Australian perspective this can be seen as part of a collaborative cultural construction where the knowledge of events and the 'ownership' and guardianship of individual family stories and histories need to be negotiated.

Performance context

The Dreamers was a huge success and Andrew Ross approached Wendy Blacklock at the Australian Elizabethan Theatre Trust to commission Davis to write another play for the 1985 Festival of Perth. *No Sugar* (the second in the *First Born Trilogy*) under the direction of Andrew Ross and with original music and choreography by Richard Walley premiered at the Maltings for the 1985 Festival of Perth. The play was then chosen to be Australia's entry at the Expo '86 World Theatre Festival in Vancouver in 1986 and was revised and remounted with a cast that included Ernie Dingo in the role of Jimmy. In 1988, it was presented in London at the Riverside Studios and in that same year it won an Australian Writers' Guild Award and the Ruth Adney Koori Award.

Also in 1986, Davis was appointed Artistic Director of the Marli Biyol Theatre Company in Perth and *Barungin* (the last play in the *First Born Trilogy*) premiered at the Perth and Adelaide Festivals under the direction of Andrew Ross. The first performance of the complete *First Born Trilogy* took place at the Fitzroy Town Hall in Melbourne in May 1988 (supported by the Melbourne Theatre Company and the Western Australian Theatre Company).

Davis went on to write other plays such as *In Our Town, Wahngin Country* and *Moorli and the Leprechauns*. His dramas, particularly *No Sugar* and the other plays in the *First Born Trilogy*, are part of a rich landscape of Australian Indigenous theatre which started with Kevin Gilbert's *The Cherry Pickers* in 1968, progresses through to Davis' *No Sugar* in the mid-1980s and continues through works such as Eva Johnson's *What Do They Call Me?* (1990), Jimmy Chi and the Kuckles Band's *Bran Nue Dae* (1990), Wesley Enoch and Deborah Mailman's *The Seven Stages of Grieving* (1997), Jane Harrison's *Stolen* (2000), Tony Briggs' *The Sapphires* (2003), Steve Hawke's *Jandamarra* (2009) and Scott Rankin and Big hART's *Namatjira* (2012).

GENRE, STRUCTURE & LANGUAGE

Genre

Playwrights do not necessarily create a piece of theatre in a specific genre. Often a playwright has in mind a set of ideas or characters or a message and then a theatrical style or genre emerges as dominant in the piece, and this may be emphasised through the influence of other writers or the contributions of a director or even actors with whom the playwright is working.

One possible description of the genre of *No Sugar* is as a naturalistic, historical-based political drama. It has been said that from a 'white' Western perspective, *No Sugar* is a protest play but from Indigenous Australian perspectives the play could be considered an historical documentary or docudrama. The use of an ordinary Indigenous Australian family and naturalistic language to explore extraordinary historical events and happenings makes the play both a documentation of social history and a form of political social commentary.

Broadly speaking, the play's genre is political drama, a didactic (intended to teach or inform) *Lehrstücke* play in the tradition of Bertolt Brecht's *The Mother*. Some people have described the play as being almost like **Brecht's epic theatre** in its style but while it is dialectical (instructional) in its approach and uses short episodic scenes, other elements of the play are definitely not epic in their style. While the play is at times overtly political, the dialogue is very naturalistic and there is no real alienation effect (from devices that prevent the audience from engaging with the characters on a purely emotional level). This means that while *No Sugar* could be described as Brechtian in its stylistic influences, it is not overtly Brechtian or epic in its style.

Certainly Davis had read Brecht's poetry and some of his plays, and his writings on theatre as a vehicle for social change. Davis' close working relationship with director Andrew Ross meant that Ross' knowledge and use of Brechtian techniques in workshops and rehearsals would have also influenced the way that *No Sugar* deals with such significant social events as the forced removal of individuals, families and whole communities.

The play might also be classified simply as **Australian Indigenous Theatre**. Some Indigenous commentators believe that the sense of community and 'portrayal of family as community' act as a collective character within Indigenous drama and this collectivity is one hallmark of Australian Indigenous Theatre. They argue that this and self-deprecating humour are major genre signifiers of Australian Indigenous Theatre (Johnson 1988, pp.12–13), and certainly these are both present in *No Sugar*.

Overall, the political aspects, naturalism of the dialogue and elements of Indigenous Theatre serve to make the play a hybrid form which spans the continuum from social realism to political protest drama.

Structure

The episodic structure of *No Sugar* reinforces the metaphoric use of space in the play: both features symbolise the division between the oppression imposed by white society and the oppressed Indigenous culture through a sense of boundaries and controls. Structurally, dramatic contrast is sometimes achieved in the play through parallel actions in scenes. Act One, Scene Two contrasts the effects of the Great Depression on people from different worlds and social groups. This multi-layering and shifting of perspectives allows the scene to foreshadow events at Moore River later in the play.

No Sugar is divided into four acts and two dominant settings – Act One and Act Three are primarily set in the Government Well Aboriginal Reserve outside Northam, and Acts Two and Four are predominantly set in the Moore River Settlement. The episodic structure of the play and the use of short scenes in each act are dramatically effective in the play's overall structure. The play employs the following five major elements of classical dramatic structure:

- **rising action**
- **climax** (the turning point)
- **falling action**
- **catastrophe**
- **catharsis**.

The first nine scenes in Act One show the progressive **rising action** that centres on the exposition of Indigenous Australians on the fringe of a white colonialist Australian culture – a culture represented by Sergeant Carrol and Neville, the Chief Protector of Aborigines. In terms of dramatic structure, Act One flips back and forth between scenes situated in the world of the Indigenous Millimurra-Munday family and those set in the non-Indigenous world. The scenes set in the Indigenous world of the Millimurra-Mundays are naturalistic and domestic, giving a sense of the world of Indigenous families as normal and identifiable to an audience. This can be juxtaposed with the structural cross-cutting which Davis uses when exploring the antagonistic white world of bureaucracy and power. Nowhere is this more evident in the play than in Act One, Scene Two (pp.11–18) and Act One, Scene Seven (pp.34–9).

The first structural **climax** in the play comes at the end of Act One in Scene Ten when the Millimurra family are moved off the Government Well Reserve (pp.44–6). This leads dramatically into the **falling action** stage of the play through Acts Two and Three, ending in Act Four, Scene Five when at the 1934 Moore River Settlement Australia Day celebrations, Indigenous people break into a parody of the religious hymn 'There is a Happy Land' (p.93). After this we enter the **catastrophe** section of the play with Jimmy having a heart attack (p.94).

Structurally, the catharsis of the play starts with Joe arriving back two weeks early from gaol; gathers momentum with Mary demanding to leave Moore River; and ends with Joe and Mary finally leaving to return to Joe's homeland in Northam with their new baby, Jimmy.

Language

The raw naturalistic language of *No Sugar* helps to give the play some stylistic elements of another genre: **naturalism**. Davis loved the plays and short stories of the Russian writer Anton Chekhov (1860–1904). What seems to have directly influenced Davis' playwriting is Chekhov's economic use of language and dialogue to create an atmosphere of poignant trivialities and authenticity where characters gain depth through their faults and weaknesses.

The language of *No Sugar* not only shapes and defines the characters in the play but serves to shape the themes, world, views and values explored in the play. There are four major types of language used in *No Sugar*. **Australian colloquial language or everyday spoken Australian language** is used throughout the play mostly for Indigenous characters but also for sympathetic white Australian characters such as Frank Brown, the out-of-work farmer. This serves to increase the realism of Indigenous characters and their trials by situating them in a language and a world that a modern audience can identify and empathise with. Davis' use of language therefore can be seen to make a modern audience feel more affinity with the concerns and values of the Indigenous characters and more specifically the Millimurra-Munday family.

A second type of language used in the play is **pejorative** (strongly negative) in its tone and vocabulary. This is spoken by characters such as Sergeant Carrol when he refers to Indigenous men as 'abos'. While the characters use this type of language to denigrate Indigenous people, on another level, Davis uses it to ironically stereotype some 'white' Australian attitudes so as to make a social comment on the relationship between language, prejudice and power.

The third type of language used is of a **non-naturalistic style**. It uses theatrical conventions such as overly formal language, as well as idioms and colloquialisms to attempt to represent and construct stereotypes. This reinforces Davis' clever use of archetypal characters and caricatures to construct many of the white characters as merely playing supporting roles alongside the play's focus on Indigenous characters and historical events. This ironic reversal of traditional roles (focusing on Indigenous instead of white characters) serves to emphasise the themes of power and oppression evident in the play. For example, Frank Brown uses colloquial words such as 'bloke' which, although initially seeming naturalistic and everyday, theatrically function to place his character within the recognisable stereotype of the 'laid-back Aussie male'. The fact that Frank Brown (a white character) uses this casual language helps to illustrate one function of colloquial language in Australian society: an egalitarian leveller which seeks to break down power in terms of class and race.

Neville, in contrast, uses language bound by other conventions throughout the play. The authoritative tone and formality of his speech sometimes serves to document and reinforce the racist, condescending and ultimately cruel acts committed by white authorities towards Indigenous people, such as those described in Neville's speech to the Royal Western Australian Historical Society (pp.80–1). Sometimes Neville's language (particularly in letters and telephone conversations) acts to both establish and mock his position of power and authority. His character has a detachment and sense of disconnection (both physically and ideologically) from the people and events being represented in the play, and his words often become more potent through this sense of formality and alienation. This is evident when, in Act One, Scene Two, he proposes cuts to the rations and sustenance for Indigenous people living on reserves under his control: 'the proposed budget cut of three thousand one hundred and thirty-four pounds could be met by discontinuing the supply of meat in native rations' (p.14).

The crucial fourth type of language used is the **Indigenous Nyoongah language**. This is evident at points such as in Act One, Scene Five when at the courthouse Sam explains to the JP 'He's my *gnoolya*' (p.31), which the Sergeant explains means brother-in-law. The primary dramatic function of the use of Nyoongah in the play is to create a cultural identity for the Indigenous characters and community; its secondary function is to alienate non-Indigenous audiences from aspects of Indigenous culture and Indigenous characters in the play.

This alienation or distance serves to make some moments more dramatically potent since audiences who have found the everyday colloquial language familiar are suddenly distanced from the Indigenous characters and their world. This distance can help audiences consider the historical events presented and the function of dispossession (of language, land and culture) on the Indigenous peoples of Australia.

A third function of the Nyoongah language in *No Sugar* is to shift the power base to the Indigenous characters. When the white characters, along with the audience, hear words from the Nyoongah language, a brief role reversal takes place and non-Nyoongah-speakers are dispossessed of language and understanding just as Indigenous Australians were dispossessed of their land and language and made to feel powerless when Europeans first colonised Australia.

SCENE-BY-SCENE ANALYSIS

Act One, Scene One: Northam (pp.9–11)

Summary: *The Millimurra-Munday family are suffering under extreme poverty at the Government Well Aboriginal Reserve.*

The play opens at the Government Well Aboriginal Reserve outside Northam early one morning in 1929. David and Cissie Millimurra play cricket with a homemade bat and ball. This signifies the simple existence that people like the Millimurra family have forged for themselves despite living on a reserve during hard times. The older brother Joe reads in the newspaper about a special centenary celebration where 'Aborigines' were 'dancing ... to a brass-band' (p.10). Their uncle Jimmy Munday is angry that Indigenous people would dance at a white celebration for the day that the 'bastards took our country' (p.10).

This sequence establishes Jimmy as not only a main character but as an intelligent Indigenous man who is not afraid to speak his own mind. Milly Millimurra gives her son David her last two pence so that he and his sister can buy apples for lunch. David's brother Joe gives him another three pence so that he can buy a pie. Milly asks her husband Sam and her eldest son Joe to go out and kill some rabbits for dinner. Joe takes a *dowak* (throwing stick or boomerang) with him.

This opening scene sets up the social status and relationships of the Millimurra-Munday family. They are poor and feeling the effects of the Depression already but are content. They kill rabbits for food, showing both their poverty and their ability to be self-sufficient. Jimmy is shown to be both intelligent and politically outspoken. In a sense, his character takes on some attributes of objective commentary during the scene; for example, he questions why Indigenous people would dance at a celebration of a time when 'them bastards took our country'. Joe is also shown to possess a connection to his culture.

Q How are both poverty and resilience represented in this scene?

Act One, Scene Two: Northam; Neville's office in Perth (pp.11–18)

Summary: *Frank Brown has arrived in the town and is questioned by the police.*

The use of a split scene or cross-cutting technique at this point serves to show the separation between the world of Neville, where abstract decisions are made, and the real everyday life of the Indigenous people who suffer the consequences of these decisions. The scene starts later on the same day in Northam. Frank Brown, an unemployed farmer who arrived a fortnight ago looking for work, is questioned by Sergeant Carrol about whether he sold alcohol to Jimmy Munday the previous Friday night. Jimmy had been paid three pounds for fox scalps on Friday but was apprehended drunk in Bernard Park later that night. Carrol points out the punishment for supplying alcohol to 'natives' is three months of hard labour in gaol in Fremantle. This establishes Sergeant Carrol as a character who is representative of those people in positions of white authority who will follow and implement the rules and regulations while having some insight into the larger picture. Frank is evasive but he doesn't admit or deny that he might have helped Jimmy.

Frank's poverty and his enforced state of wandering about looking for work, along with the distinct possibility that he has flaunted the law and supplied alcohol to Jimmy, sets up him as a character whose circumstances have increased his sympathy towards Indigenous people. Frank is reprimanded by Carrol who claims that he has 'nothing against' Indigenous people but he knows 'exactly what they're like' (p.13). Davis cleverly sets up two white attitudes to Indigenous people: one like Frank's that understands and empathises with Indigenous people, and another like Sergeant Carrol's which shows some tolerance hidden behind prejudices and preconceptions.

The scene then cross-cuts to Perth where Neville and his secretary Miss Dunn discuss the thirty percent unemployment rate and the difficulty of these times but the ingenuity of some 'white' people. This admiration soon becomes ironic as Mr Neville makes notes to himself about how cutting rations to the 'natives' could make the Department further savings. This shows Neville as representative of an authority and bureaucracy that does not acknowledge the circumstances and basic humanity of the Indigenous people under their control. Neville rings Sergeant Carrol in Northam to discuss moving the natives from Government Well to another site. Neville tells the Sergeant that because of objections by white people, the Lands Department has recommended that the Aborigines should be moved to another site 'well away from any residences'.

Key point

This telephone sequence shows that authority figures like Neville wish to keep themselves removed and distant from Indigenous people. As Neville hangs up, he goes back to his bureaucratic world.

Meanwhile, back in Northam, the Sergeant signs over government rations to Gran and Milly including flour, sugar, tea and a very small package of meat and dripping. It is these provisions that they rely on but as the rations are depleted one by one, they will realise they don't need the 'sugar' or enticements of 'white' handouts to survive and thrive. Sergeant tells Milly that soap is no longer included in the ration and when she complains, Sergeant suggests that Jimmy, Sam and Joe should all be working. The Sergeant threatens that he will lock Jimmy up the next time he sees him.

We cross-cut back to Perth where Neville dictates a letter to Miss Dunn which he wants sent to Neal (the superintendent of the Moore River Native Settlement) commending him on the state of the settlement but showing his concern for the 'dirty little noses amongst the children' and his desire to see 'each child issued with a handkerchief'. This is ironic, particularly because we are starting to see the effects of the ration reductions for which Neville is responsible.

Q Why has Davis used cross-cutting (moving between locations/ realities) in this scene? What is its function?

Act One, Scene Three: Northam (pp.18–25)

Summary: *Frank Brown comes to the Millimurra-Munday family's camp to have dinner. He supplies alcohol to Jimmy and Sam.*

David and Joe play two-up with bottle tops while Cissie cooks damper on the fire. Jimmy enters with Sam and Frank Brown who Jimmy has befriended. Milly and Gran return; Gran puts onions and potatoes in the camp oven and Jimmy produces some turnips he has taken from somewhere. Milly warns Jimmy that he will end up in Fremantle Gaol again. Jimmy asks Frank if he has ever been in 'Freeo' gaol, saying that he himself has been there four times already.

Over dinner, Frank relates how he lost his farm to the bank. Jimmy tells Frank that it is worse for Indigenous people because they are not even allowed to walk the streets of town at night because of the curfews. Then Sam and Jimmy get into a fight after Jimmy accidentally hits Joe in the nose. Gran separates them and tells Sam to get off Jimmy because he is 'sick in the chest' (p.25). Milly pours Jimmy's bottle of port wine on the ground. Gran's mention of Jimmy's heart condition is significant since this is the first time the audience hears about this; it suggests a vulnerable side to Jimmy, despite his defiance of white oppression, and foreshadows his death near the end of the play.

Q Why is it important that women are the ones shown to stop the men from creating trouble?

Act One, Scene Four: Northam (pp.25–8)

Summary: *Sergeant Carrol and Constable Kerr arrest Jimmy and Sam for drunkenness.*

Later that night, Jimmy and Sam are put in the Northam Police Station lockup for drinking and the Sergeant wonders who gave Jimmy the bottle of port wine. Jimmy takes out a mouth organ and plays 'Home, Sweet Home'. This tune is ironic, signifying a sense of home and belonging evident in Jimmy even though he is very much dispossessed of his home at this moment.

The police demand for Jimmy to give up the mouth organ can be seen as a foreshadowing of the enforced relocation of Jimmy and his family at the end of Act One from Northam to the Moore River Settlement. Jimmy surrenders his mouth organ to the Constable, but continues to be disruptive, complaining about a hole in the toilet bucket and throwing the bucket across the cell. The Sergeant threatens Jimmy with six months in gaol and decides to add 'damage to government property' to Jimmy's charges (p.27). Jimmy sings an Al Jolson song from a recent film he saw and muses at why a white man was 'makin' out he was black' in a movie (p.28).

This is paradoxical since it shows how white culture accepts its own superficial representations of 'black' society while rejecting the 'black' society it finds on its own doorstep. Jimmy asks if the Sergeant has told Gran and Milly that he and Sam have been locked up. The Sergeant ignores Jimmy's question and goes off to interview publicans to see if he can find out who gave Jimmy the 'grog'. This shows not only a disregard for Jimmy and his family but also a disregard for procedure and the law.

Q What is ironic about a white man like Al Jolson putting on black make-up and, as Jimmy says, 'makin' out he was black' (p.28)?

Act One, Scene Five: Northam (pp.28–31)

Summary: *Jimmy and Sam are charged and sentenced for drunkenness; Frank is charged with supplying alcohol to Indigenous men.*

At the courthouse in Northam the next morning, Frank, Jimmy and Sam are brought before the Justice of the Peace (a local farmer). Frank admits to supplying alcohol but points out how he felt obliged to do it because Jimmy and his family were very kind to him. Frank's attitude is shown to be reasonable but he is still punished. Frank is charged with supplying alcohol to natives and is sentenced to six weeks imprisonment with hard labour, a signal of a society that harshly punishes 'white' people who mix with Indigenous people. Jimmy is sentenced to three months imprisonment with hard labour for various offences and Sam given a fine that he must pay within fourteen days or also risk imprisonment.

Q Why do each of the three men charged receive such different sentences?

Act One, Scene Six: Northam (pp.32–3)

Summary: *Cissie becomes sick.*

It is now winter at Government Well. Jimmy is still in gaol. Food is scarce; Joe can't even trap rabbits. All there is to eat is damper. Cissie is sick with a fever. Sam is busy trying to make money fencing so he can pay off his fine. Joe goes to get Uncle Herbie's horse and cart to take Cissie straight to the hospital.

Q How do poverty and isolation create a sense of potential for tragedy in this scene?

Act One, Scene Seven: Northam; Neville's office (pp.34–9)

Summary: *Jimmy gets out of gaol; Milly and Gran discover rations have been further cut.*

It is early on a winter's morning in 1932; Jimmy is out of gaol and waits for Mr Neville so that he can get a voucher for the train ticket home to Northam. Neville is telling Sergeant Carrol on the phone that there are problems with finding a place for a new 'native reserve' to move the Indigenous people of Northam onto. Neville leaves it with the Sergeant to come up with another alternative. The mention of it being too late to 'adopt the Tasmanian solution' (p.39) is a flippant joke with sinister undertones which refers to the attempted extermination of Tasmanian Indigenous people. Jimmy finally gets his train voucher for the eleven o'clock goods train but he says he is now in no rush and will take the five o'clock Kalgoorlie train instead. This dialogue is comic and gives a sense of Jimmy as a stereotypical 'likeable larrikin'.

At the same time, Gran and Milly arrive at the police station in Northam and try to get their rations from Sergeant Carrol. Rations have been further reduced and meat is no longer on the ration list. They also ask for blankets for Cissie for when she comes out of hospital but are told that blankets can't be provided.

Q What is ironic about the Sergeant's comment about the 'Tasmanian solution' in light of the diminishment in government care and sustenance given to the Northam Indigenous community?

Act One, Scene Eight: Northam (pp.40–1)

Summary: *Jimmy comes home.*

On Jimmy's return to Government Well Reserve, he is upset to hear that meat has been taken off the ration list. We see that it is Jimmy who stands up for the rights and dignity of his family and people. Many in his family have resigned themselves to their fate. Joe goes to borrow a cart and horse from Skinny Martin to pick up Cissy. Jimmy plans to steal a sheep from Skinny Martin for dinner; Gran warns Jimmy of the consequences if he is caught, but Jimmy doesn't listen. Jimmy's actions here suggest his strong capacity for resourcefulness – even if it involves breaking the law.

Act One, Scene Nine: Neville's office (pp.41–3)

Summary: *Neville asks the Sergeant to organise moving the Indigenous people of Northam to Moore River Settlement.*

It is almost Christmas and Sergeant Carrol arrives in Perth at Neville's office. In this scene we see the bureaucratic handling of Indigenous people meet with the enforcement of these decisions on the ground. A decision to move all of the 'eighty-nine natives' (p.42) from Government Well to the Moore River Settlement is being rushed through, supposedly because the local Indigenous inhabitants are 'rotten with scabies' (p.42). However, the real reason seems more likely to be political: there is mention of how the timing is connected to an upcoming election. Neville insists that the inhabitants be moved with very few possessions and that no dogs are to be taken with them.

Q How does this scene show the level of hypocrisy in the bureaucracy of the time?

Act One, Scene Ten: Northam (pp.44–6)

Summary: *Sergeant Carrol serves a warrant on the Millimurra-Munday family to move them to Moore River.*

Sergeant Carrol arrives and, somewhat predictably, is met with resistance from Jimmy. Although Jimmy can't vote, he shows he knows about the election and the political reasons for moving his people. Jimmy is told he will go by train because he has a heart condition and Gran is told that she will also travel by train because of the length of the journey. Gran insists she wants to go with Milly and the rest of the family by road with the spring cart. This signifies Gran's strength of will and the extent to which she values family.

The Sergeant allows Gran to go by road and, worn down by their complaints, he also allows them to take their dogs. It is significant that Act One ends with a sense of inevitability about the Millimurra-Munday family's loss of home and their forced removal: this echoes across many years of policies and mistreatment of Indigenous Australians.

Key point

Davis carefully portrays Jimmy as worldly, intelligent, politically aware and informed about the real reasons for the shifting of the Indigenous people. This actively challenges stereotypes of Indigenous people.

Q Why does the Sergeant accede to Gran's demands?

Act Two, Scene One: The track to Moore River (pp.49–51)

Summary: *The Millimurra family arrive at the Moore River Settlement and meet the tracker Billy Kimberley.*

Arriving at the Moore River Settlement, the Millimurra-Munday family meet Billy Kimberley, a black tracker who introduces himself initially as a 'politjman', though in fact he only works with the police and is not actually an employee. Billy later becomes a strong symbol of an Indigenous person caught between two worlds.

Jimmy, who has already arrived, shows his family where to go for food, and then goes off to 'find' them a sheet of metal for a fireplace, once again showing that his ability to provide for the family is not necessarily bound by morals.

Q Why does Billy introduce himself initially as a 'politjman'?

Act Two, Scene Two: Moore River (pp.51–3)

Summary: *Joe is introduced to Mary and they decide to arrange another meeting.*

While Joe, David and Cissie are filling water bags down at the river, Joe meets Topsy and Mary Dargurru and he arranges to meet Mary at the same place the next day. This is a beautiful scene that paints a familiar picture of attraction between two young lovers. An audience, regardless of race or culture, can likely relate to the awkwardness and serendipity of this meeting.

The discussion of Uncle Herbie's connections to the two families reinforces the importance of extended kinship networks in linking Indigenous people together and contributing to a sense of identity.

Q Why does Davis have this significant meeting happen while the characters are collecting water?

Act Two, Scene Three: Moore River (pp.53–5)

Summary: *Matron checks the Millimurras for scabies and finds they have no signs of it.*

Matron Neal comes with Mary and Topsy to check the Millimurra family for scabies. She finds them all healthy and comments on what a strapping lad Joe is. In the course of her examination, Matron Neal's findings allude to the fraudulence of the cover story about why the Indigenous families have been relocated.

Act Two, Scene Four: Moore River (pp.56–7)

Summary: *Joe and Mary meet at night; she reveals the abuse perpetrated by Neal on the community.*

Joe and Mary meet and confess their love for each other. Mary also tells Joe about the darker side of Mr Neal, and his tendency to behave inappropriately and cruelly towards the girls in his charge. The revelations of Mr Neal as 'always hangin' around the girls' establish him as immoral and an antagonistic force within the drama; they also help motivate Joe's decision, several scenes later, to escape with Mary.

Q How does this scene dramatically juxtapose despair and hope?

Act Two, Scene Five: Moore River (pp.57–9)

Summary: *Jimmy confronts Neal with the lies about the quarantine camp and widespread scabies.*

After Jimmy confronts Neal, Matron confirms the fact that the quarantine camp is a scam. Mr Neal ignores all this and seems concerned that the new arrivals have brought so many dogs. This scene reinforces the notion that many people like Mr Neal turned a blind eye to the lies that were used to justify the forced relocation of Indigenous people.

Act Two, Scene Six: Moore River (pp.59–65)

Summary: *The Millimurra-Munday men organise a gathering and Jimmy sings to Billy and Bluey; Billy describes the 1926 massacre in his homeland; Joe meets Mary again.*

In this scene, Billy laments that the few survivors of his people all left their home country after a massacre. This is a potent reminder of the long history of massacres of Indigenous people.

They all hear a noise and disperse except for Joe who has arranged to meet Mary there. They kiss. Then Mary tells Joe that Mr Neal wants her to work in the hospital – where he has a particular reputation for abusing girls in his charge. Joe and Mary decide to run away back to Northam.

Key point

It is significant that Joe finds the strength to stand up for Mary and himself immediately after a traditional ceremony and sharing of stories. We see here that singing, dancing and stories function like a rite of passage into manhood for Joe.

Q How does this scene give a sense of why Billy lives in the shadows between his own culture and the non-Indigenous world?

Act Two, Scene Seven: Moore River (pp.65–6)

Summary: *Joe tells his family that he and Mary plan to run away.*

Joe wakes his parents and Jimmy and tells them what he has learned about Mr Neal, and reveals he wants to run away with Mary back to Northam. It is pointed out that Mary is a 'compound girl'. The sense of the artificial divisions that 'white' society places on Indigenous people is subtle but potent. Milly gives Joe and Mary some food and wishes them luck.

Q How does this scene create a feeling of hope and renewal?

Act Two, Scene Eight: Moore River (pp.67–8)

Summary: *Neal hears that Joe and Mary have run away; he sends Billy after them with a whip.*

Matron Neal tells her husband about Joe and Mary running away together and she mentions that it is because Mary was afraid to work in the hospital. It is significant that Matron Neal insinuates that she knows of Mr Neal's immoral dealings with Indigenous women. Mr Neal sends Billy after them and allows him to take a whip.

Q How is the whip seen as a symbol in the play of white power and aggression? What is the significance of Neal giving it to Billy at this point?

Act Two, Scene Nine: Near Mooloombeeni (pp.68–70)

Summary: *Joe and Mary encounter Billy by the train tracks but escape.*

Joe and Mary are waiting by the train tracks to take the train back to Northam when Billy arrives; he attempts to whip them and arrest them. Joe grabs the whip and handcuffs Billy. Joe and Mary escape on the train.

This scene demonstrates that although Billy is able to carry the symbols of white power and abuse, he is somehow unable to use them against Joe and Mary. This emphasises his position between the two worlds – his experience doesn't align cleanly with one or the other of the cultures. (Note that this scene is incorrectly labelled 'Scene Ten' in the play script.)

Act Two, Scene Ten: Moore River (pp.70–2)

Summary: *Billy returns to tell Neal that he allowed Joe and Mary to escape.*

When Billy arrives back at Neal's office, Neal is angry that Billy has allowed Joe and Mary to escape on a train. Significantly, Matron shows concern for Billy and it is she who is able, through gesturing, to get an answer out of Billy about which way the train was heading. While Neal insists on using language – which clearly isn't working – to try to get the information out of Billy, Matron takes an alternative approach and has more success. Neal takes Billy to the blacksmith to get the handcuffs off; the scene ends with Matron trying Indigenous food.

Q Matron tries *quandong* at the end of the scene. What does this symbolise?

Act Three, Scene One: Northam (pp.74–5)

Summary: *Joe and Mary arrive at Northam, only to find everything has been destroyed and burnt.*

Although they encounter destruction at Northam, Joe is at least able to find a couple of workable rabbit traps.

Q How does this scene show devastation but also suggest hope and the possibility of survival?

Act Three, Scene Two: Northam (pp.75–6)

Summary: *Joe and Mary are questioned by the Sergeant about why Joe has come back and where they are staying.*

In Northam, Joe and Mary meet Sergeant Carrol who questions them. Joe expresses his anger at all the property being destroyed. The Sergeant warns them to stay away from the Government Well site.

Q What does this sequence show us about Joe that was not obvious before?

Act Three, Scene Three: Northam; Neville's office (pp.76–8)

Summary: *The Sergeant rings Neville in Perth to decide what to do about Joe and Mary and is told to serve warrants on them both.*

Neville tells Sergeant Carrol that he should serve warrants on Joe and Mary and since Mary is a minor, that Joe should be arrested and sent to gaol for absconding with a minor. The Sergeant finds some old warrants to serve on them. The advice of Neville and the actions of the Sergeant show the disdain with which both administrators and police treat Indigenous people and the law.

Act Three, Scene Four: Northam (pp.79–80)

Summary: *Joe is arrested by the Sergeant.*

Joe doesn't resist arrest, but nor does he agree to being handcuffed when he is taken away, showing both his selfless concern for Mary and his desire to retain his dignity despite impending imprisonment. He tells the Sergeant to let Mary know where he is.

Q How would you describe Joe's attitude to being arrested?

Act Three, Scene Five: Perth (pp.80–1)

Summary: *Neville gives a talk to the Royal Western Australian Society on the history of contact with Indigenous people.*

With a portrait of the King, the Union Jack and the Western Australian flag behind him, Neville delivers a speech on the history of the 'protection' of 'natives' in Southern Western Australia. He mentions the massacres of 'natives' almost as though they were necessary, and almost applauds the fact that nearly half of the native population are 'half-caste'.

The tangible symbols of European settlement on the wall behind Neville serve to position him further in the imperial past, reminding us that his attitudes towards the natives are anything but progressive.

Key point

Although Neville's speech is serious, its function in the play is both humorous and ironic, as it allows the audience to laugh at Neville's statements while being appalled by his attitudes.

Q How does Davis use historical material (such as the text of the speech) to make a comment on attitudes and values?

Act Four, Scene One: Moore River (pp.83–6)

Summary: *Cissie and David attend Sunday School to get sweets.*

All of Act Four is set at the Moore River Native Settlement. In this scene, Sister Eileen is running Sunday School and Topsy is shown to be submissive, obedient and knowledgeable, retelling aspects of Bible stories. At the end of Sunday School, the children sing the hymn 'There is a Happy Land'.

The hymn singing can be seen as part of a religious indoctrination which dispossesses Indigenous people in this life, while promising them glory in the next. Later (in Act Four, Scene Five) the Indigenous community ironically turns this hymn into a form of deviant protest.

Key point

This is the primary scene in the play that shows the dealings of religious people and missionaries with Indigenous Australians. The Church is shown as caring and benign but blindly optimistic.

Q What does this scene show about the role and place of religion in some Indigenous communities?

Act Four, Scene Two (pp.86–7)

Summary: *Mary is brought into Neal's office; we find out she is pregnant; she refuses to obey Neal, and is whipped by him.*

When Mary enters Neal's office, he insists that Mary must go to work in the hospital, but she refuses to obey him. This act of defiance is both a symbol of Mary's independence as an adult and a sign of her need to stand up for herself and other Indigenous people. Billy holds Mary down while Neal beats the pregnant Mary with his whip.

Q What is the significance of Billy holding down Mary while Neal beats her?

Act Four, Scene Three (pp.87–9)

Summary: *Mary goes to stay with Joe's family and is embraced as one of the family.*

Mary stays with Joe's family and she wants Gran to deliver the baby. Her beating at the hands of Neal has strengthened her resolve. A letter from Joe, who is in Fremantle Gaol, is read out. Joe knows about the baby and mentions his intention to marry Mary when he is released.

Q How is a sense of renewal and hope evident in this scene?

Act Four, Scene Four (pp.89–91)

Summary: *Sister Eileen visits Neal in his office to discuss the preparations for the Australia Day celebrations in Moore River.*

It is significant that the celebrations will involve Mr Neville, the Chief Protector of Aborigines, coming up from Perth. We also see tension between Neal and Sister Eileen on how to deal with the 'natives'. Neal sees submission, violence, ignorance and illiteracy as a solution and even threatens to send Sister Eileen to a more remote location.

Q How and why does Davis encourage us to relate to Sister Eileen's attitudes more than to Neal's?

Act Four, Scene Five (pp.91–4)

Summary: *At the Australia Day celebrations, Mr Neville gives a speech; the Indigenous inhabitants parody the hymn; Jimmy speaks out about the reality facing his people and then has a heart attack.*

Neville's speech is about the benefits and prosperity that he thinks colonisation has brought to the native population. Sister Eileen leads them all in the singing of the hymn 'There is a Happy Land' but after this the Indigenous people break into a parody verse which points out the reality of their oppression. Mr Neville expresses how appalled he is by this display. When Jimmy speaks out about the reality of his people's situation, the political machinations and lies about scabies, he is eventually driven to have a heart attack.

Key point

This can be seen as the climax of *No Sugar* since it brings together most of the worlds of the play – Mr Neville's, Mr Neal's and Sister Eileen's, as well as the world of the Millimurra family and Jimmy Munday: Indigenous people who have faced starvation, forced removal and even gaol but still live in dignity.

Q How does bringing together the worlds of the different characters give the climactic events in this scene more dramatic impact?

Q Some critics see the singing of the parody verse of the hymn 'There is a Happy Land' as a moment of defiance, whereas others see it as an act of resignation. Which do you think it is, and why?

Act Four, Scene Six (pp.94–6)

Summary: *Jimmy has died and Neal shows little empathy for the Millimurra family.*

Sam and Milly plead with Neal for permission for Joe to be allowed out of gaol for his uncle's funeral. Neal refuses, saying they can tell Joe about the death in a letter. Even at this moment of deep grief for the Millimurra family, Neal lacks empathy for them.

Q Why at the end of the scene does Milly appeal to Matron for a proper coffin for Jimmy?

Act Four, Scene Seven (pp.96–8)

Summary: *Mary goes into labour and Gran safely delivers the baby boy.*

When Gran delivers Mary's baby we see Mary embrace her new Indigenous family. Matron arrives and Mary is distressed because she doesn't want Matron to take the baby away. Before she leaves, Matron commends Gran on the good job she has done in delivering the baby.

Q What is the significance of having Mary's baby delivered by Gran?

Act Four, Scene Eight (pp.99–101)

Summary: *Joe arrives back two weeks early from gaol; he names his baby son Jimmy after his uncle; Joe sees that Mary has whip marks and they decide to seek permission to leave Moore River.*

Joe has used the money he made working in gaol to buy gifts for everyone, including a red dress for Mary. It is significant that when Joe sees his baby son, he wants to name him Jimmy after his dead uncle; in this way, Jimmy will be remembered and honoured by the next generation.

When Mary tries the dress on, Joe notices the scars on Mary's back from where she was whipped by Neal. Joe wants to take revenge out on Neal but Mary says that they should demand to leave the Moore River Settlement instead. She says that Matron will also stand up for them against Neal.

Q What are the messages put forward by the events in this scene?

Act Four, Scene Nine (pp.102–4)

Summary: *Neal agrees to allow Joe and Mary to leave the settlement.*

Neal agrees to Joe and Mary leaving but gets Joe to sign a document that promises that he won't return to Northam. Joe signs the document and Billy, even though he is illiterate, witnesses the document. Billy gives Joe a parting gift of the whip to kill rabbits and snakes.

Q Billy says to Joe, 'That your country. You back sit down that place' (p.103). What is the significance of Billy saying this and giving Joe the whip as a parting gift?

Act Four, Scene Ten (pp.104–5)

Summary: *Joe and Mary leave for Northam. The Millimurras give them parting gifts and they leave with Gran singing a song in her traditional language.*

Milly gives Mary a sugar bag filled with provisions and utensils for their journey. Sam then asks Joe where they will go, and Joe states that he intends to go back home to Northam with Mary and baby Jimmy. A magpie squawks, the totem of their homeland. Gran sings as they leave.

Q What is the symbolism of Joe and Mary being given a sugar bag that is filled with supplies rather than sugar?

Q What is the significance of Gran singing a song in an old language as Joe and Mary set off to seek a new life in Joe's homeland?

CHARACTERS & RELATIONSHIPS

Jimmy (James) Munday

Key quotes

'You fellas, you know why them *wetjalas* marchin' down the street, eh? I'll tell youse why. 'Cause them bastards took our country and them blackfellas dancin' for 'em.' (p.10)

'They can shoot our dawgs, anytime they want to. Bastards. They shot Streak.' (p.23)

'Fuck you, you white bastard, fuck you.' (p.28)

'… that's why we got dragged 'ere; so them *wetjalas* vote for him … So he could have a nice, white little town …' (p.93)

Jimmy is the major protagonist of *No Sugar*. He is the son of Gran Munday, the brother of Milly Millimurra and uncle to Joe, David and Cissie. As an Indigenous Nyoongah man in his forties, he represents a bridge between the traditional culture and a forthright activism. In Jimmy, Davis seems to advocate that activism is what has helped Indigenous Australians to survive through years of oppression and suppression.

Jimmy knows the machinations of 'white' people in power, and functions as the voice of reason and protest through his words and actions. This is most evident in Act Four, Scene Five when, during the Australia Day celebrations, Jimmy argues with Mr Neville about the conditions, food and treatment of Indigenous people even though this outburst eventually leads to him dying of a heart attack (pp.94–5).

Jimmy can be seen as a tragic figure not only because of his death but because of the nobility of his nature. His death on one level represents the loss of voice and protest of Indigenous peoples to the power of white colonialism, but on another level it symbolically marks the passing on of his voice and protest to his descendants Joe Millimurra and Joe's newborn son who is named after Jimmy as a tribute.

Key point

An audience can relate to the humour and modernity of Jimmy's character. This humour shows itself in the way he talks back to white men in positions of authority and it could be said that humour is one of the few weapons Jimmy has to attack authority.

Gran Munday

Key quotes

'Don't worry, we can use *tjeerung* bush. I know where some growin'.' (p.20)

'Chergeant, I'm not leavin' Wow Wow behind. If I can't take him, I'm not goin'.' (p.46)

'… put these *jeerung meear* on your back. Fix up quick and make you better.' (p.87)

'I got you a little Nyoongah. Now I cut your cord … Now cover you in ashes. More better than Johnson's Baby Powder, eh?' (p.97)

Gran is the mother of Jimmy Munday and Milly Millimurra and the grandmother of Joe, David and Cissie. She is wise, knowledgeable, traditional and functions in the play not only as a strong matriarchal figure and backbone of the family but also as someone who embodies and is able to pass on the more traditional ways of her family, tribe and Indigenous culture. Age and hardship have made her open and unafraid to voice her opinions.

Gran is tough and stands up to Sergeant Carrol when Neville cuts the rations of the Indigenous people and when the Sergeant wants to take her by train to the Moore River resettlement. She also delivers Mary and Joe's baby.

Gran speaks predominantly in everyday colloquial language and is able to survive and provide for herself and her family off the land even at times of hardship.

Milly Millimurra

Key quotes

'Here's twopence, you can buy an apple each for lunch.' (p.10)

'You wait till brother Jimmy hears about this no soap business.' (p.17)

'Don't wake the kids. Less they know the better.' (p.66)

Milly is the sister of Jimmy Munday and daughter of Gran Munday. She is married to Sam Millimurra and has three children, Joe, David and Cissie. Her love and her concern for looking after her family are shown through her giving her last coins to her younger children for apples for their lunch and her telling her older son Joe and her husband Sam to go out and get a couple of rabbits because meat rations are diminishing (p.11). This sense of care for her family is also demonstrated when she complains to Sergeant Carrol about soap being taken out of the rations (pp.16–17).

In some ways she is reliant on the men in her life, specifically her brother Jimmy and her husband Sam. Davis frames Milly primarily within the domestic context but she is not passive and even chastises Jimmy when he gives her stolen food for a stew, suggesting that such theft will eventually put Jimmy in gaol (p.21). Her dominant traits are that she is maternal, unselfish, self-sacrificing and driven by a sense of equality even though she seems ultimately resigned to her situation.

Milly is also shown to be strong at a number of points in the play. When the family arrives at the Moore River Native Settlement after a long journey, it is Milly who gets the family organised (pp.50–1). Although she worries about her family, this does not prevent her from offering her support for them when they want to do what they feel is right or what makes them happy. An example is when she offers her reluctant blessing to Joe sneaking off with Mary when Mary and Joe first leave for Northam (p.66).

It is the death of Jimmy that prompts Milly to stand up for herself and her family, and she even threatens Mr Neal when he refuses to ring the prison to tell Joe about the death of his uncle (p.95). She shows further courage when she helps deliver Mary's baby and when she speaks up to tell Joe that it was Neal who whipped Mary (p.101).

Sam Millimurra

Key quotes

'What, leave the dogs behind?' (p.46)

'Come on, Milly, we get Cissie to write to him. Come on, Milly. Come on, come on now.' (pp.95–6)

Sam is the husband of Milly Millimurra and the brother-in-law of Jimmy Munday. He looks up to Jimmy (even though they sometimes fight) and, early in the play, follows him even when it involves breaking the law. He loves his family, hunting and his dogs.

Ultimately, Sam is relatively passive and not as outspoken as his wife or his brother-in-law, except when it comes to speaking up against leaving the dogs at Northam before travelling to Moore River. After Jimmy's death he becomes more scared of anyone standing up to white authority figures like Superintendent Neal. In some ways he acts as a counterpoint in the play to both Jimmy and Joe who stand up for what they believe in, despite the consequences.

Joe Millimurra

Key quotes

'You eat underground mutton before?' (p.22)

'Don't need no dawg. Don't need no shoes either, Granny, I can run better barefoot and faster than Wow Wow.' (p.41)

'He's a strapping lad.' (p.55)

'I wanna call him Jimmy.' (p.100)

Milly and Sam's eldest son, Joe is about eighteen years old and can read. In the play he represents the new generation (in the 1930s) of Indigenous Australians. He is a survivor and is willing to take on the roles of hunting and providing even as a young man. Unlike characters such as Topsy and even his father Sam, he does not accept the controls of life at the Moore River Mission and he fights for justice on an individual level.

Joe falls in love with Mary and learns to speak up for himself and others. In his independence and resilience he has attributes similar to Jimmy and Gran Munday. He is adventurous and takes responsibility when he follows Jimmy's advice to 'jump a rattler' (p.66) and run away with Mary back to Northam. He is then arrested for absconding with a minor and spends six months in Fremantle Gaol.

Joe's romantic relationship with Mary and his connection to his family and heritage are strengthened throughout the play. By standing up for Mary and eventually going back with her and their newborn son to Northam, he can be seen to symbolise a hope and independence for younger Indigenous people that is anchored not just in traditional beliefs and inheritance of culture and land, but in commitment, family and fighting for one's beliefs.

Key point

The dramatic function of Joe in the text is interesting: it is possible to see Joe as representing the journey from childhood to manhood, and it is his connection to his culture which facilitates this journey.

Mary Dargurru

Key quotes

'I don't care. You can belt me if you like, I'm not workin' in the hospital ... Go to hell! Fuck youse!' (p.87)

'You're not havin' my baby, leave him alone!' (p.98)

'He got wild 'coz I wouldn't knuckle under to him. Don't go, Joe, not now. Go on Monday and ask him if we can leave the Settlement.' (p.101)

Mary is an Indigenous girl of about sixteen, from the Kimberley region, who works with Matron Neal and falls in love with Joe Millimurra. When we first meet Mary it seems that her destiny may be similar to Topsy's – one of submission and subservience – but we see her grow in confidence and defiance as she falls in love with Joe and becomes pregnant.

Mary's strength is illustrated when she challenges Mr Neal, swears at him and is able to endure him beating her with a cat-o'-nine-tails even though she is pregnant with Joe's baby (pp.86–7). She moves in with the Millimurra family and wants to have Gran deliver the baby rather than go back to the hospital. She fears her baby will be taken away and even killed. It is interesting to note that it is Mary who is the driving force behind preventing Joe from taking violent revenge on Mr Neal and she is the one who suggests that Joe, she and the baby leave the Moore River Settlement.

Billy Kimberley

Key quotes

'[*poking his whip at* DAVID] You shut up now.' (p.53)

'Big mob *gudeeah*. Big mob politjmans, and big mob from stations, and shoot 'em everybody mens, *koories*, little *yumbah*.' (p.62)

Billy Kimberley is an Indigenous tracker in his twenties from 'up North' (the Kimberley region) who works for Mr Neal and carries a whip. Billy speaks in simple English interspersed with some Indigenous Kimberley words. Ironically, after the massacre of his people (the Oombulgarri Massacre) which he describes in Act Two, Scene Six (pp.61–3), Billy is the one who Mr Neal gets to enforce discipline against other Indigenous people. He even belts Indigenous children with his whip to keep them in check during Sunday School (pp.83–4).

Billy can be seen as a strong symbol of the battle between heritage and survival experienced by many Indigenous people in the twentieth and twenty-first centuries. Billy is taunted by Indigenous people and even the children label him a traitor or 'black crow' (p.84). It is a touching symbolic moment at the end of the play when Billy gives his whip to Joe and tells him to 'back sit down' in his country (p.103).

Key point

Davis constructs Billy as a significant minor character who is torn between the loss of his Indigenous culture (he is the last of his tribe) and his work for the corrupt colonialist white Australia (as represented by Superintendent Neal). Billy is representative of many Indigenous people caught in such situations.

Auber Octavius Neville

Key quotes

'... the proposed budget cut of three thousand one hundred and thirty-four pounds could be met by discontinuing the supply of meat in native rations.' (p.14)

'... if you provide the native the basic accoutrements of civilisation you're halfway to civilising him.' (p.18)

'I'm appalled by this disgraceful demonstration of ingratitude ... There will be no privileges from now on ... And there will be no Christmas this year!' (p.93)

Mr Neville is the Chief Protector of Aborigines, a bureaucrat in his early fifties who has control over the lives and conditions of Indigenous people in Western Australia during the time in which the play is set. His secretary is Miss Dunn. Neville's formal and condescending statements and phrases thinly disguise the devastating effects of his control of the affairs of Indigenous communities, such as the Government Well Aboriginal Reserve at Northam and the Moore River Native Settlement. His character ultimately comes across as a pompous caricature of white colonialism.

Key point

Neville, the character, is not only based upon the real historical figure of Auber Octavius Neville, but the real Neville's speeches and statements are sometimes used as speeches in the play. The use of actual historical material in a dramatic context can help us question the authority and accuracy of written historical materials.

Superintendent Neal

Key quotes

'He's always hangin' around where the girls are workin'; in the cookhouse, in the sewin' room. And he's always carryin' that cat-o'-nine-tails ...' (p.56)

'You bloody incompetent savage.' (p.72)

'Millimurra seems to have learnt her well. Well, I'm going to unlearn you.' (p.87)

Mr Neal is the superintendent at the Moore River Settlement, and is married to Matron Neal. He does not like Indigenous people and wants to keep them in their place. He does not even believe that Indigenous people should be encouraged to read (p.90). He is a cruel, unsavory character who regularly becomes drunk and violent. He is lecherous around young Indigenous girls and he tries to get them transferred to areas like the hospital so he can physically and sexually assault them (p.56). Neal sees Indigenous people as savages who need to be beaten and suppressed in order to become civilised.

When Mary is brought back to Moore River Native Settlement after running away with Joe, Neal is warned by his wife that Mary is pregnant and unwell. This does not stop him as he grows progressively more furious when Mary swears at him and refuses to follow his demand that she go and live in the nurses' quarters. He then grabs the pregnant Mary and whips her with a cat-o'-nine-tails to 'unlearn' her (p.87).

Matron Neal

Key quotes

'I think she was scared of the living.' (p.68)

'As matron in charge of the hospital, I thought it was my job to allocate nursing aides.' (p.68)

'Don't worry, he'll receive a proper burial.' (p.95)

Matron Neal is married to Neal and is the local Matron for the Moore River Settlement. Her character has direct parallels to Gran in that both women are the backbones of their communities. She is wise, calm and caring: a kind maternal figure who looks after, and is the true protector of, the Indigenous people in her Moore River community – particularly girls like Mary and Topsy.

Matron Neal's attitudes and beliefs about Indigenous people can be directly contrasted to those of her husband. Her presence in the play raises questions about whether people of compassion who allow others to perpetrate crimes and great wrongs are in some way complicit or responsible for such wrongs. Around her husband, she fluctuates from being guarded to being lighthearted and forthright. She sees that kindness, good health and education will ultimately be the answer to improving the lives of the Indigenous people and thus acts as a symbol of the hopes of some white Australians for freedom and justice for Indigenous Australians.

Sergeant Carrol

Key quotes

'Take it from me, I been dealin' with 'em for years. I got nothin' against 'em, but I know exactly what they're like.' (p.13)

'Your trouble, Milly, is you got three healthy men bludging off you, too lazy to work.' (p.17)

> 'Just make yourself scarce and don't go campin' anywhere you're not s'posed to be …' (p.76)
>
> 'Haven't had any bother with them. Millimurra's working at Lockyers, they're not collecting rations.' (p.77)

Sergeant Carrol is the local sergeant in Northam. A police officer in his forties, he is officious but not cruel. He has some sympathy for Indigenous women like Milly and Gran and even tries to be helpful to them (p.37); he gives in to Gran when she wants to take a dog with her to Moore River (p.46). The Sergeant thinks most Indigenous men are lazy and openly expresses his poor opinion of them, but he tolerates Joe when he comes back to Northam because Joe has found work at Lockyers (p.77). Jimmy, though, is a different story; Sergeant Carrol does not like or even tolerate Jimmy and even bends the truth to have Jimmy locked up (pp.30–1).

Sister Eileen

Key quotes

> 'The Lord Jesus Christ has sent His servant, Mr Neville, Chief Protector of Aborigines, to speak to us on this special day.' (p.91)

Sister Eileen is a nun who runs the Sunday School at Moore River Settlement. In her thirties, she is religious and believes in education rather than punishment. As a character in the play, she represents Davis' sympathetic view towards religion. She comes across as naive and slightly condescending, treating most Indigenous people, from teenagers to adults, as if they were children. Her ignorance and refusal to acknowledge the actual conditions and treatment of Indigenous people by people like Neal and Neville seems to come from a religious blindness and her belief that God is providing all necessary 'sustenance in life' (p.91).

Minor characters

Cissie Millimurra

Cissie is Milly and Sam's daughter, in her early teens. She helps her mother by doing odd jobs like collecting water (p.51) and even plays cricket with her brother (p.9). She enjoys teasing Joe when she finds out that he has a girlfriend (p.52).

David Millimurra

David Millimurra is the youngest son of Milly and Sam. He likes to play cricket and idolises Don Bradman, the famous white Australian cricket player (p.9).

Topsy

Topsy is Mary's subservient and submissive friend who also works for the Matron. She is already a convert to Christianity, eagerly showing off her rote learning of religious stories and figures in Sunday School (p.83). In this, she provides a strong contrast to Cissie, who shows no knowledge of or interest in the Bible stories but is much more closely connected to her family.

Frank Brown

Frank is an out-of-work farmer in his forties. He befriends Jimmy, giving him alcohol after Jimmy provides Frank with a meal and the loan of a razor. 'Associating with natives' and supplying alcohol to them causes Frank to be sent to gaol for six weeks with hard labour (pp.29–30).

THEMES, IDEAS & VALUES

Injustice and violence

Key quotes

'... it's been decided to transfer the entire native population to the Moore River Settlement.' (p.42)

'He's always hangin' around where the girls are workin' ... he's always carryin' that cat-o'-nine-tails and he'll use it, too ... My friend went last Christmas and then she came back *boodjarri*.' (p.56)

'Big mob politjmans, and big mob from stations, and shoot 'em everybody mens, *koories*, little *yumbah*.' (p.62)

'Well, I'm going to unlearn you. [NEAL *grabs her*. BILLY *holds her outstretched over a pile of flour bags*. NEAL *raises the cat-o'-nine-tails* ...]' (p.87)

'And that's why we got dragged 'ere; so them *wetjalas* vote for him ... So he could have a nice, white little town ...' (pp.93–4)

The issues of injustice and violence against Indigenous Australians are themes that are dealt with through many, if not most, works of modern Australian Indigenous drama. Specifically, *No Sugar* highlights the injustices of the period of control and 'protection' policies instituted across most Australian colonies. These policies were administrated by the Aboriginal Protection Boards and injustices were exacerbated when some governments began to sell off parts of Aboriginal reserves. The expansion of the granting of pastoral leases led to the extension of the powers of Aboriginal Protection Boards, which in turn led to police being given power and control over most Indigenous peoples. The values displayed through these behaviours are those of a 'white' sense of cultural and social dominance and power.

The reasons why and the ways in which the Indigenous community of Government Well have their rations cut and their meat ration discontinued are portrayed in the play as being not only unjust (pp.14–17) but also a tool of political machinations (p.93). Further injustices are illustrated when the Millimurra family and others are forcibly removed from their Northam homes to the Moore River Native Settlement under the false pretext of a scabies outbreak (pp.42–3).

In Act Two, these injustices are compounded with stories of the physical and sexual violence perpetrated on young girls by Superintendent Neal, who does not even believe that Indigenous people should be taught how to read (p.90). There are even stories of infanticide being committed and it is suggested that Neal is behind these horrors. These stories are placed in a wider context of violent persecution and destruction when in Act Two, Scene Six, Billy Kimberley tells of the 1926 Oombulgarri Massacre in his homeland in the Kimberley region. Billy relates that men, women and children were killed and their bodies were burnt and then thrown into the river (pp.61–3). His story is just one reminder of a long history of massacres perpetrated against Indigenous peoples by white colonisers.

Davis further reinforces his portrayal of injustice and violence against Indigenous people when he confronts his audience with more violence. When the pregnant Mary stands up to Superintendent Neal in Act Four, Scene Two, saying 'You can belt me if you like, I'm not workin' in the hospital' (p.87), Neal then grabs her and, with the help of Billy, beats her with a cat-o'-nine-tails. The idea embodied here is that Indigenous Australians have the bravery and resilience to stand up to inhumane and violent treatment.

This bravery is seen again when all of the Indigenous people in the Moore River Native Settlement revolt against their diminishing food rations and the increasing diet of religious fervour by parodying a Christian hymn during the 1934 Australia Day celebrations visited by the Chief Protector of Aborigines, A. O. Neville.

Racism

Key quotes

'Not abos or half-castes?' (p.12)

'I seen that talkin' picture at the Palace, sittin' right up the front, the roped off section for blackfellas.' (p.28)

''Coz *wetjalas* in this town don't want us 'ere, don't want our kids at the school, with their kids …' (pp.44–5)

No Sugar addresses the theme of racism on many levels. From the arrival/invasion of British colonialists to the conflicts, war, genocide and government policies of Protectionism and Control, the play suggests that racism and supremacist values underpin the white treatment of Indigenous peoples. Racism was practised against Indigenous people on governmental, cultural and personal levels.

One of the first examples of discrimination we encounter in the play is the illustration of the ways in which white bureaucracy and government policy were prejudiced against Indigenous people during the Depression. The Millimurra-Mundays are shown to be malnourished, receiving only basic rations and no supply of clean water for household use (p.10 and pp.50–1).

The Indigenous people of the Northam community are not given the same rights of freedom of movement as the white people in their community. As Jimmy mentions to the unemployed white farmer Frank, 'you know we're not allowed in town, not allowed to go down the soak, not allowed to march' (p.23). This segregation and control of Indigenous people's movements extends to where they are able to live, and they are even put behind a rope at places like the cinema (p.28). The values and ideology of white racial superiority are thus embedded in official policies and laws.

On a more interpersonal scale, the Indigenous characters are subject to racism on the level of verbal abuse. They are called derogatory names such as 'abos' (p.12). The Millimurra-Munday family and other Indigenous people in the Northam community are under constant surveillance from the police. They are forbidden to drink alcohol and are even denied proper wages for the work they do, as evidenced when Sam's work for Skinny Martin is paid for with an old pair of boots and tough meat (p.17). Racism also means that contact between Indigenous and white people is limited and controlled: Frank Brown is questioned by Sergeant Carrol for drinking with and befriending the Millimurra-Munday family and 'hangin' about with natives' (p.12).

By showing the ways in which racist attitudes and discrimination divide the white and Indigenous societies, Davis is able to construct characters who must battle against prejudice and oppression. Gran, Jimmy Munday and Joe Millimurra are able to identify, question and challenge these attitudes and finally to rise above racism. This can be seen, for instance, when Jimmy declares to Neville, 'You come an' eat supper with us, tonight, right? Bread and drippin' and black tea. Are you game to try it?' (p.93).

Indigenous identity

Key quotes

'Nyoongahs corroboreein' to a *wetjala*'s brass band!' (p.10)

'And you fellas, we got no meat for dinner or supper; you'll have to go out and get a couple of rabbits.' (p.11)

'*Karra koorliny, karra koorliny, karra koorliny, / Woolah!* ... That's my grandfather song.' (p.60)

Aboriginal and Torres Strait Islander or Australian Indigenous identity is a theme which is dealt with both subtly and overtly throughout *No Sugar*. Indigenous Australian culture and identity are characterised by a fusion of the social, the material and the spiritual. Davis' play reinforces the message that even after experiencing poverty, racism and abuse the Indigenous identity is able to survive if links to family (as represented by the Millimurra-Munday family) and a sense of place (as suggested by Joe's return with Mary and his baby son Jimmy to Northam) are maintained or re-established.

While a popular misconception is to situate Aboriginal and Torres Strait Islander identity in the outback, the island life or the 'Dreamtime', Davis gives us a much more complex notion of Australian Indigenous identity. He centres the narrative of the play primarily on the Millimurra-Munday family who live on the fringe of Australian society. In fact, the primary 'outback' Indigenous person represented in the play is Billy Kimberley (the Indigenous tracker who works for Mr Neal), who is shown to be caught between his Indigenous identity and the social role he performs in white society as an enforcer of violence and control over Indigenous families on the Moore River Native Settlement.

In this sense, Davis makes an audience and a reader of the play question their notions of Indigenous identity since he demonstrates that Indigenous identity cannot be entirely centred in the distant past. It is ultimately their connection to the values of tradition, the land and family which makes the Millimurra-Mundays survivors, and this is the underlying viewpoint expressed by the play, for both non-Indigenous and Indigenous audiences.

Key point

The primary source of the conflict and tension in *No Sugar* derives from the inability of most whites in the three major worlds of the play (Government Well, Neville's office in Perth and the Moore River Native Settlement) to admit to and acknowledge a different perspective and value system and to seek dignity through understanding.

For some characters, such as the Sergeant, this occurs because of preconceptions that many Indigenous people (particularly males like Jimmy) are lazy and are a burden on the system. Sadly, this type of judgemental attitude still exists today because, like the Sergeant, some cannot see that Indigenous Australians are often not given the same opportunities as other people.

Notions of Indigenous identity are addressed in *No Sugar* not only through a contrast with the white or Anglo-Australian attitudes and customs but also through interactions between different Indigenous characters. The play starts with the Millimurra-Munday family drinking tea (laced with sugar at this point in the play), playing cricket and reading the newspaper. From one perspective, this could be read as a representation of their loss of identity and their assimilation of white customs and ways. However, their assimilation of these customs is mediated by a number of things:

- the fact that the bat is homemade
- the way Milly casually asks the 'fellas' to 'get a couple of rabbits' for dinner (p.11)
- the way Jimmy openly criticises 'Nyoongahs corroboreein' to a *wetjala*'s brass band' (p.10) (at the centenary of Western Australian Indigenous peoples' dispossession mentioned in the newspaper).

This shows that Indigenous people like the Millimurra-Mundays have survived because they are resourceful and openly able to criticise the hypocrisies of the world around them.

Yet their resourcefulness and ability to adapt and incorporate new customs does not mean that the Indigenous characters have lost their connection to the past. In a powerful sequence in Act Two, Scene Six, in a clearing in a pine plantation, the Indigenous men of the Moore River Native Settlement – including Jimmy, Sam, Joe and even Bluey and Billy – paint themselves, sing, dance and tell stories in a corroboree-like ceremony or sharing. When Jimmy sings his grandfather's song about crabs and fish in his traditional Nyoongah language (p.60), Billy and Bluey are impressed.

We see here that a connection is made between Indigenous people from different regions through the song. The fact that Jimmy is able to sing the song in the language of his ancestors brings admiration from others.

In this sense, the passing down of language as well as dances and song are seen as having great value in terms of Indigenous identity. These types of rituals provide a common ground and reflect the value of finding a point of common understanding for these Indigenous men from different generations and places.

Possession and dispossession

Key quotes

'... you know we're not allowed in town ...' (p.23)

'... it's been decided to transfer the entire native population to the Moore River Settlement.' (p.42)

'... all male persons between the ages of fifteen and fifty were required to enrol in the militia, to secure the safety of the territory from invasion and from the attacks of hostile native tribes ...' (p.81)

No Sugar is a powerful critique of the dispossession and destruction of Indigenous culture and identity caused by colonial expansion. By concentrating on a specific family (the Millimurra-Mundays), a specific tribal clan (the Nyoongah) and a specific historical period and event (the Great Depression and the forced removal of the Indigenous people from Government Well to Moore River), the play is able to explore dispossession, attempted assimilation and the ultimate marginalisation of Australian Indigenous peoples.

The play demonstrates that dispossession is not just a feature of colonialism and imperial attitudes, and nor does it relate only to taking Indigenous people away from their homelands. Rather, dispossession comes through a conscious attempt by individuals and authorities to systematically eliminate a culture and a way of life. Thus we can see possession and dispossession to be not only an issue of land and the ability of a people to provide for and sustain themselves, but a more complex issue that is linked to cultural inheritance and a sense of belonging.

On one level, most white characters can be seen as trying to bring their own civilisation to what they see as primitive Indigenous people; on another level, they can be seen as initiating and carrying out a systematic program of cultural dispossession and destruction. In the case of Sister Eileen, this takes place when the Church dispossesses Indigenous children of their stories and spiritual beliefs, barraging them instead with Christian stories and traditions. In Sergeant Carrol's case, enforcing the actual removal of Indigenous people from their homeland is a more physical form of dispossession.

On a larger scale, Mr Neville can be seen as a symbol of a system that consciously and maliciously seeks to destroy Indigenous Australian society. He is representative of people in power and a bureaucracy not only committed to dispossessing Indigenous people of their homeland, but depriving them of reasonable sustenance and causing the systematic breakdown of their families, livelihoods and culture. He is part of the system that also endorses the slaughter and decimation of Indigenous lives and culture that he mentions in his speech to the Royal Western Australian Historical Society (pp.80–1).

Davis shows that this decimation was not only enacted on a governmental and bureaucratic level; many ordinary white people also perpetrated acts of cruelty and dispossession. This is evident in the horrific story told by Billy Kimberley of the slaughter of his people at the Oombulgarri Massacre (pp.61–3). Billy's story is significant in the play because Billy is shown to have lost not only his land, his people and his family, but also his identity. His sense of identity exists neither in the Indigenous world of his homeland in the Kimberley, nor in his place as a tracker for the violent Mr Neal at Moore River.

Key point

If Billy is the successful product of assimilation then he becomes the ultimate argument against it. He doesn't remember his language, he doesn't remember any traditional knowledge and he is reduced to becoming a helper and enforcer of violence against other Indigenous people.

Poverty

Key quotes

'... we got no meat for dinner or supper; you'll have to go out and get a couple of rabbits.' (p.11)

'... the proposed budget cut of three thousand one hundred and thirty-four pounds could be met by discontinuing the supply of meat in native rations.' (p.14)

Many people consider that poverty is the major issue which still prevents Australian Indigenous peoples from maintaining dignity and achieving an increase in living standards comparable to other Australians. From the early days of colonialism, Indigenous peoples were dispossessed of their lands and were placed in a dire predicament.

The relocation and attempted control of Indigenous people on reserves and missions complicated the issue. By losing their land, their freedom, their lifestyle and any chance of a livelihood, Indigenous people were thrown into the cycle of poverty illustrated in *No Sugar* with the Millimurra-Munday family. They are shown to be far more disadvantaged and impoverished than non-Indigenous people during the Great Depression. They have to beg for the ever-decreasing rations which are their right by government laws (p.16) and even soap becomes a luxury (p.17). They have to supplement their meagre rations by hunting for rabbits (p.11) and stealing vegetables (p.21). This situation is made worse when they are moved to the Moore River Native Settlement.

At Moore River, the Millimurra-Mundays are confronted with a soup kitchen which serves them meagre meals which include treacle and bread, or bread and fat; their ability to find and cook food for themselves becomes severely limited (pp.50–1). Later in the play, it seems that the only regular rations they are getting are flour and tea. The gifts that Joe brings back, bought with the income he earned working while he was in Fremantle Gaol, are a welcome relief from the family's hard existence.

Although some white characters, such as Sergeant Carrol, express the belief that Indigenous people only live in poverty because the men are 'bludging' and 'too lazy to work' (p.17), Davis dispels this myth through Sam Millimurra, who is a hard worker but is often only given tough meat or old boots in payment for hard labour (p.17). Other signs of exploitation are shown throughout the text, especially when it is revealed that thirty out of eighty Indigenous girls who were sent from Moore River into domestic service returned pregnant, presumably molested by their white bosses.

Ultimately, however, *No Sugar* is not simply a tale of the poverty, dispossession and exploitation of Indigenous people, but could be considered a story of hope. The play gives us hope, for example, that when Joe, Mary and their baby Jimmy return to Northam at the end of the play, Joe will find work and he and Mary will once again be able to support themselves as they did the first time they went to Northam.

Family

Key quotes

'How can I keep my kids clean and sen 'em to school?' (p.16)

'Ay, Mill, he's married; got three kids and a wife.' (p.23)

'I ain't goin' on no train. I'm goin' with Sam and Milly.' (p.45)

'I wanna call him Jimmy.' (p.100)

Through the hardships, dispossession and poverty experienced by the Indigenous characters in *No Sugar*, family and links to the land give hope and identity to Indigenous characters. Initially the Millimurra-Munday family are shown to be bound together by the fact that they live together as an extended family of three generations – Gran; Jimmy and Milly; Joe, Cissie and David.

The hunting, gathering and making of food, the collection of water and the creating of a fire are family activities to which everyone seems to contribute (pp.9–10). They look after one another and seem to have a particular commitment to looking after the children, making sure they have good food like apples for lunch (p.10) and that there is soap so that the children can go to school clean (p.16). They even feel sorry for Frank Brown when he reveals that he has not seen his family for six months (p.24). Even though there is an occasional fight between some members of the family, such as the drunken fight between Jimmy and Sam which is broken up by Gran (pp.24–5), they look after one another, as illustrated when Sam tries to calm down Jimmy while they are locked up in the Northam police cells (p.27).

The suppression and control of their lives by government and police authorities does not succeed in severing the bonds of family that keep the Millimurra-Mundays together. Although they are forcibly moved from their homelands in Northam to Moore River, their strong family bonds enable them to maintain their sense of identity even when they have lost their land and sense of place. Gran doesn't want to travel on a train to Moore River and be separated from Milly, Sam and the children, so she wails and cries until the Sergeant relents (p.46).

When Joe and Mary try to leave Moore River for the first time, their night-time escape is given the support of Joe's family with advice and provisions such as damper and a blanket (p.66). Even Joe being locked up in gaol does not break the bond of their family, and Cissie reads Joe's letter from gaol out aloud even though it contains swearing (pp.88–9). When Mary has her baby, she does not want Matron's help, but wants her baby to be delivered by Gran, the matriarch of her new family. Mary waits until Joe returns from gaol to name the baby and Joe picks the name Jimmy in honour of his recently deceased uncle (p.100).

At the very end of the play, when Mary and Joe are preparing to return to Northam (violating the agreement Joe signed for Mr Neal), Mary calls Milly 'Mum', reinforcing that Mary has also found a sense of belonging to her new family. The play ends with Joe, Mary and baby Jimmy going off to the sounds of magpies (the totem of the Millimurra-Munday family) and in the old language Gran makes their journey into a new song to be carried into the future.

DIFFERENT INTERPRETATIONS

Different interpretations arise from different responses to a text. Over time, a text will give rise to a wide range of responses from its readers, who may come from various social or cultural groups and live in very different places and historical periods. Responses by critics and reviewers can be published in newspapers, journals and books, both online and in print. They can also be expressed in discussions among readers in the media, classrooms, book groups and so on.

While there is no single correct reading or interpretation of a text, it is important to understand that an interpretation is more than a personal opinion – it is the justification of a point of view on the text. To present an interpretation of a text based on your point of view you must use a logical argument and support it with relevant evidence from the text.

The critics' viewpoints

No Sugar was a critical, popular and financial success when it was first performed at the Maltings for the Festival of Perth in 1985. The play's powerful portrayal of the trials, tribulations, survival and resilience of the Millimurra-Munday family struck a chord not only with festival audiences but also with subsequent audiences throughout Australia. It was seen as a strong story of one family's survival and, to non-Indigenous audiences, it gave an insight into the resilience of Indigenous people and families under what essentially was control, forced removal, segregation and apartheid. It also challenged popular myths and portrayals of Indigenous people as 'happy people who live in the outback' or 'a race that is fading away peacefully' (Casey 2004, p.150).

In this sense, some critics saw the power of *No Sugar* in 1985 in the context of the beginnings of the breakdown of apartheid in South Africa (which started with South African Government negotiations with Nelson Mandela in 1985). *No Sugar* in this context can be seen as part of a process of reconciliation; it asked non-Indigenous audiences to acknowledge the past injustices, dispossession and hardship enacted on Indigenous people in Australia. As one critic suggested:

> *No Sugar* was portraying life under the Apartheid Acts of the 1930s and 1940s to audiences conditioned by the assimilation Acts of the 1960s and 1970s and undergoing a transition towards multiculturalism in the 1980s. (Casey 2004, p.152)

The theatre practitioner and critic John Callum places Jack Davis' plays, like Kevin Gilbert's *The Cherry Pickers*, Robert Merritt's *The Cake Man* (1975) and Gerald Bostock's *Here Comes the Nigger* (1975), within the genre of realism of the 1970s and 1980s. Aboriginal and Torres Strait Islander academic Clifford Aidee Goori Watego saw the play as being situated within an extreme naturalism which has an 'intense preoccupation with producing real life situations' (Watego 1990, p.11).

Certainly, the success of the play initially could have been due to its realism and the sense that audiences were being given a privileged insight into Indigenous people's lives being lived on stage using what Davis himself described as a conscious performance choice to show 'the behavioural patterns and speech patterns of Aboriginal people'. Watego identifies as central to the play its 'intense preoccupation with reproducing real life situations'. *No Sugar* can be seen as sitting within a canon of Indigenous Australian drama of the 1970s and 1980s which is essentially domestically realist in style. But this denies the historical context of the events portrayed in the play, and thus makes non-Indigenous audiences merely voyeurs to the lives of an Indigenous family. In this sense, the success of the play should have diminished over time as its exoticism dissipated. However, the power and appeal of *No Sugar* goes beyond its realistic portrayal of the Millimurra-Munday family.

The original Andrew Ross production of the play was performed in the oppressively humid and hot venue of the Maltings in an open performance area. This performance space allowed the audience to move with the actors from Northam to the Moore River Native Settlement. The set was dominated by Brechtian elements such as harsh floodlights, slogans and the thick bars of a gaol. These Brechtian elements were toned back for the touring production of the show and the World Theatre Festival version offered in Vancouver, Canada.

Many people have since criticised the stylistic elements of Ross' original production, but it must be remembered that Ross worked very closely with Davis on the development of the original play and it is obvious that the political content was vital to both Davis and Ross. It could be said that the Brechtian stylistic elements of Ross' original production were an attempt by a non-Indigenous theatre director to come to terms with the political elements of this play. Ross may also have used Brechtian techniques as a political and theatrical entry point that would be well understood by his predominantly non-Indigenous audience.

Ross' production of *No Sugar* can be contrasted with the 1994 production by Indigenous director, actor and playwright Bob Maza, whose direction emphasised the more naturalistic elements while allowing the political and symbolic elements to emerge more subtly. While *No Sugar* initially was portrayed as a political protest play and then a naturalistic historical-based docu-drama, its strong message and moving characters have allowed it to move on to allow different interpretations in different performance contexts.

Two interpretations

Interpretation 1: *No Sugar* is a representation and critique of the violence towards and cultural destruction of Indigenous people under Protectionism.

This interpretation sees *No Sugar* as essentially a protest play which realistically portrays the effects of government policies on one Indigenous family as a way of critiquing the devastating effects of such policies on Indigenous peoples in general. The narrative can be seen as a journey through poverty, dispossession and marginalisation to eventual survival for one Indigenous family who represent the broader Indigenous experience at this time.

The white representatives of colonial authority endeavour to bring their version of civilisation to the Indigenous people. Yet, in doing so, they effectively use their power in an attempt to systematically destroy the Indigenous people by:

- cutting their rations and means of existence
- dispossessing them of their land and heritage
- enacting bureaucratic decisions without thinking of the effects on the Indigenous groups and families involved
- jailing young Indigenous males
- perpetrating individual and systemic acts of violence
- using religion to indoctrinate and make illegitimate the spiritual and cultural beliefs of Indigenous peoples
- trying to control and stop the movement of Indigenous people back to their land, thus depriving them of their cultural place, sense of identity and link to their ancestral inheritance.

This interpretation offers a postcolonial perspective which sees the play as portraying resistance against the attempt to systematically dispossess and destroy Indigenous identity and culture.

Textual evidence that supports this interpretation includes the following:

- In the first scene, the main Indigenous characters perform everyday 'white' Australian activities (playing cricket, reading a newspaper); their adoption of non-Indigenous culture can be seen as a form of social and cultural control – a symbol of dispossession.
- The use of hybrid English/Indigenous language throughout the play by the Indigenous characters symbolises the alienation of the Millimurra-Munday family both from their own culture and language and from the colonialist British culture and language.
- The Millimurra-Munday family display resistance and rejection of the 'white' European culture. They parody the religious hymn on Australia Day (p.93), and Jimmy's sharpening of an axe in the

opening of the play can be seen as a potent symbol of the sharp weapons of survival, family and identity, which the Millimurra-Mundays will fight with.

- Davis' use of historical speeches and documents from A. O. Neville invites the audience to question the dominant voices and ideologies which determine history and people's lives. This is further reinforced by the moving retelling of the 1926 Oombulgarri Massacre by Billy (pp.61–3).
- The driving force of tension behind the play is the power and sense of superiority of 'white' people and their culture, and the active rejection of this cultural imperialism: a rejection characterised by Jimmy's statement, 'them bastards took our country and them blackfellas dancin' for 'em. Bastards!' (p.10).
- The white 'protection' actually results in a systematic elimination of Indigenous ways of life. The Millimurra-Mundays are forced to move to the Moore River Settlement without most of their belongings and animals (pp.44–6); when Joe first returns to Northam with Mary, he finds the homes and belongings of the Nyoongah people destroyed (p.74).

At the end of the play, after the audience has been confronted with the harsh reality of seeing Indigenous people subjected to racism, dispossession and violence, we see Joe and Mary leaving with their baby son Jimmy to reclaim their land and culture with a pride and sense of identity that is admirable and heroic. This could be read as offering hope that the Indigenous people and cultures remain resilient, although some may also see this hope as undermined by the sense of foreboding underlying Gran's song.

Interpretation 2: *No Sugar* is ultimately a celebration of hope, culture and identity of Indigenous families.

Some critics see *No Sugar* and some of Davis' plays such as *Kullark* and *The Dreamers* as not belonging to the same movement as the social realist and protest Australian Indigenous drama of the 1970s and early

1980s, but as a precursor to the celebratory Indigenous Australian drama of the 1990s and early twenty-first century best characterised by *Bran Nue Dae* and *The Sapphires*. If we view Davis' *Kullark* as an acknowledgement of over 150 years of oppression and exploitation, and *The Dreamers* as an expression of 'what it is to be an urban Aboriginal, despite hypocrisy, untruths, and the constant pressure of the surrounding European world' (Shoemaker 1989, p.254), then *No Sugar* could be interpreted as a work about the triumph of family and individuals against the backdrop of oppression and attempts at dispossession and institutionalisation.

Many textual elements support this interpretation of *No Sugar*. For example, Davis uses historical records and information not only as research for his play but as parts of the text itself. This dramatically challenges the information, authority and 'voice' of history presented, suggesting that the play is a more contemporary work retrospectively celebrating the survival and culture of the Indigenous characters portrayed, rather than simply documenting experiences as the social realist protest plays did.

In addition to the incorporation of non-Indigenous historical voices, the use of the Indigenous Nyoongah language and the rhythms of colloquial speech give an authentic Indigenous voice to the portrayal of events. This can be seen to add an authenticity and validity to the history and events being portrayed from an Indigenous perspective, particularly in light of Indigenous history being primarily bound in culture and an oral tradition. An example is Billy's account of the Oombulgarri Massacre – a piece of history which is made more vivid and authentic by his oral telling of it. Again this provides evidence that the play is a celebration of Indigenous culture.

The irony and humour in *No Sugar* express a unique part of Australian Indigenous identity: a bittersweet honest tenderness that signals a critical reflection on the suffering endured (Shoemaker 1989, pp.255–6). This is shown in many moments in the play, from Jimmy's ridiculing of Indigenous people dancing at a '*wetjala*' (white) celebration (p.10) to the irreverent repartee of Gran and Milly with people in positions of authority (e.g. p.17).

The irony of the motif of sugar is potent both in the title and throughout the play itself. When Neville gives advice to Jimmy that 'sugar catches more flies than vinegar' (p.34), the irony is that not only do the family have no sugar, but Neville and his bureaucracy are never sweet and always bitter in their decisions involving Indigenous people. As the title of the play signals, the Indigenous characters have 'no sugar', both literally and figuratively. They only have their dignity and their humour which they sharpen like the axe Jimmy sharpens in the play's opening. They use their sharp wit at key moments, such as when they parody the religious hymn, enraging Neville in the play's climax (p.93).

The perspective offered by the play's conclusion could be interpreted as pessimistic, as indicated by the tone of Gran's song, but it can also contribute to the interpretation of *No Sugar* as a celebration of Indigenous culture and identity. In this interpretation, the play's conclusion is filled with hope as we see the Millimurra-Munday family – who have fought for survival – triumphing when Joe, Mary and their baby Jimmy leave the Moore River Settlement with the hope of a new life in the old land of Joe's ancestors. They walk towards their new life with the sounds of Gran's song both warning them of what they have to face and giving them the hope that they will forge a new future.

QUESTIONS & ANSWERS

This section focuses on your own analytical writing on the text, and gives you strategies for producing high-quality responses in your coursework and exam essays.

Essay writing – an overview

An essay on a literary work is a formal and serious piece of writing that presents your point of view on the text, usually in response to a given topic. Your 'point of view' in an essay is your interpretation of the meaning of the text's language, structure, characters, situations and events, supported by detailed analysis of textual evidence.

Analyse – don't summarise

In your essays it is important to avoid simply summarising what happens in a text.

- A **summary** is a description or paraphrase (retelling in different words) of the characters and events. For example: 'Macbeth has a horrifying vision of a dagger dripping with blood before he goes to murder King Duncan.'
- An **analysis** is an explanation of the real meaning or significance that lies 'beneath' the text's words (and images, for a film). For example: 'Macbeth's vision of a bloody dagger shows how deeply uneasy he is about the violent act he is contemplating – as well as his sense that supernatural forces are impelling him to act.'

A limited amount of summary is sometimes necessary to let your reader know which part of the text you wish to discuss. However, always keep this to a minimum and follow it immediately with your analysis of what this part of the text is really telling us.

Plan your essay

Carefully plan your essay so that you have a clear idea of what you are going to say. The plan ensures that your ideas flow logically, that your argument remains consistent and that you stay on the topic. An essay plan should be a list of **brief dot points** – no more than half a page.

- Include your central argument or main contention – a concise statement (usually in a single sentence) of your overall response to the topic. See 'Analysing a sample topic' for guidelines on how to formulate a main contention.
- Write three or four dot points for each paragraph indicating the main idea and evidence/examples from the text. Note that in your essay you will need to *expand* on these points and *analyse* the evidence.

Structure your essay

An essay is a complete, self-contained piece of writing. It has a clear beginning (the introduction), middle (several body paragraphs) and end (the last paragraph or conclusion). It must also have a central argument that runs throughout, linking each paragraph to form a coherent whole. See examples of introductions and conclusions in the 'Analysing a sample topic' and 'Sample answer' sections.

The introduction establishes your overall response to the topic. It includes your main contention and outlines the main evidence you will refer to in the course of the essay. Write your introduction *after* you have done a plan and *before* you write the rest of the essay.

The body paragraphs argue your case – they present evidence from the text and explain how this evidence supports your argument. Each body paragraph needs:

- **a strong topic sentence** (usually the first sentence) that states the main point being made in the paragraph
- **evidence** from the text, including some brief quotations

- **analysis** of the textual evidence explaining its significance and **explanation** of how it supports your argument
- **links back to the topic** in one or more statements, usually towards the end of the paragraph.

Connect the body paragraphs so that your discussion flows smoothly. Use some linking words and phrases like 'similarly' and 'on the other hand', though don't start every paragraph like this. Another strategy is to use a significant word from the last sentence of one paragraph in the first sentence of the next.

Use key terms from the topic – or synonyms for them – throughout, so the relevance of your discussion to the topic is always clear.

The conclusion ties everything together and finishes the essay. It includes strong statements that emphasise your central argument and provide a clear response to the topic.

Avoid simply restating the points made earlier in the essay – this will end on a very flat note and imply that you have run out of ideas and vocabulary. The conclusion is meant to be a logical extension of what you have written, not just a repetition or summary. Writing an effective conclusion can be a challenge. Try using these tips:

- Start by linking back to the final sentence of the second-last paragraph – this helps your writing to 'flow', rather than leaping back to your main contention straight away.
- Use synonyms and expressions with equivalent meanings to vary your vocabulary. This allows you to reinforce your line of argument without being repetitive.
- When planning your essay, think of one or two broad statements or observations about the text's wider meaning. These should be related to the topic and your overall argument. Keep them for the conclusion, since they will give you something 'new' to say but still follow logically from your discussion. The introduction will be focused on the topic, but the conclusion can present a wider view of the text.

Essay topics

1 'Jimmy Munday is a hero whose death allows others to finally take their destiny into their own hands.' Do you agree?

2 'Most of the characters in *No Sugar* are exaggerated stereotypes.' Do you agree?

3 'As a piece of social realist drama, *No Sugar* challenges social stereotypes and cultural myths.' Discuss.

4 "You can belt me if you like, I'm not workin' in the hospital ... Go to hell!"

'It is only when people stand up for themselves that they are able to rise above adversity and survive.' Discuss.

5 'Family, protest and identity are crucial for the survival of individuals.' How does *No Sugar* show this to be true?

6 'It is the women in *No Sugar* who show the greatest strength and aptitude for survival.' Discuss.

7 "And that's why we got dragged 'ere ... So he could have a nice, white little town ..."

'Many of the injustices perpetrated against Indigenous people in *No Sugar* are the result of a sense of superiority dominant in privileged "white" Australians.' Discuss.

8 How does Jack Davis use dramatic elements to explore racism, dispossession and identity in *No Sugar*?

9 "Take it from me, I been dealin' with 'em for years. I got nothin' against 'em, but I know exactly what they're like."

How does *No Sugar* show the effects of prejudice?

10 '*No Sugar* suggests that history is not only written in history books but lives in the stories and traditions of individuals and families.' To what extent is this play a social history as much as it is a piece of protest drama?

Useful vocabulary for writing on *No Sugar*

Assimilation: This policy, unofficially started in the late 1920s, aimed to culturally, spiritually and socially absorb Indigenous Australians into 'white' society through a process of suppressing Indigenous identity, culture, family and spirituality. (The policy eventually escalated in the 1930s to removing children from their families. These children became known as the Stolen Generation.) It was not until the 1970s that this policy was officially disbanded.

Dramatic irony: In a play, dramatic irony occurs when the meaning or purpose of an action, situation or speech is understood by the audience but not by the character(s).

Social realism: A movement in art and theatre which uses realistic techniques to make social commentary on working class or suppressed individuals to raise social consciousness. Social realism sometimes focuses on the ugly realities of the everyday lives of the poor and dispossessed.

Split scene or cross-cutting: This is a dramatic technique where two or more scenes are performed on stage at the same time and the action inter-cuts or cross-cuts between the various scenes. This makes it possible to juxtapose different times, places, perspectives or realities.

Analysing a sample topic

'It is the women in *No Sugar* who show the greatest strength and aptitude for survival.' Discuss.

You should always begin the process of writing an essay on a topic, prompt or question by circling any instruction words (telling you what you have to do) and underlining the key words. Here you would circle 'discuss'. Discuss means to try to cover the issues raised and not just address one side or viewpoint. Then underline 'women', 'greatest', 'strength', 'aptitude' and 'survival'.

Then take a moment to think what is meant by this question/statement in relation to the text. Use your dictionary if you do not understand any words. Jot down synonyms for these words. Write down any examples or quotes from the text you think may be appropriate.

Identify the different aspects of the statement and jot down what your main stance or arguments will be. Remember, since this statement asks you to discuss, you will probably not provide just one viewpoint or argument.

Look closely at what the statement is asserting. Here, the statement asserts that it is the women in the play who show the most strength and the greatest potential for survival. You need to understand how you are going to define strength and aptitude. You need to form your own contention (whether you agree or disagree with the statement) at this point and write it down.

Jot down four to six arguments you would make to prove your contention or argument then list the examples or proof you would use to support the arguments. If you get stuck on a statement like this, focus on a word like 'strength' or 'survival' and break down your argument by looking at different female characters to identify how they show different types of strength and how their aptitude for survival is reinforced by these strengths. It sometimes works to think of characters who are an exception to the rule, too.

Sample introduction

> Although *No Sugar* is a play that shows the destructive consequences of Control Boards, marginalisation, racism, assimilationist attitudes and policies on Indigenous Australians in the late 1920s and 1930s, it is ultimately a story of the strength and ability to survive. In particular, the women in *No Sugar* have the greatest ability to find the strength not only to ensure their own survival but to ensure the survival of others.

Outline of body paragraphs

- **Gran shows strength** in her traditional knowledge, as evidenced through her safe delivery of Mary's baby (pp.96–7) and the willpower she shows when she insists on travelling by road to Moore River to stay with her family. Eventually she ensures the survival of the family's connection to their past and their sense of identity by keeping them together. This can be contrasted with Jimmy who passes on some knowledge but ultimately does not survive.
- **Milly shows aptitude and great strength** as things become tougher for her family. She even stands up to authority figures such as the Sergeant, ensuring the physical survival of her family (p.16). You may want to use her husband Sam as a contrast since he grows progressively more passive throughout the play.
- **Matron Neal can be seen to lack the strength to stand up to her husband.** This could support an argument that although she may survive physically, her sense of identity and morality does not survive due to her inability to actively challenge her husband; an example is when she acknowledges the power her violent husband has over girls in her control (p.68).
- **Mary initially has the ability but not the strength** to stand up for herself. She eventually finds the strength to stand up to Neal (pp.86–7) and the strength to stand up for her own survival. She also ensures the survival of her baby and his cultural place and inheritance by suggesting that she, Joe and baby Jimmy leave the settlement (p.101).

Sample conclusion

> In conclusion, although *No Sugar* shows a people and a family who battle to survive all the trials to which they are subjected, it is the ability of the Indigenous females in the play that stands out. These characters, particularly Gran, Milly and Mary, find personal, familial and cultural strength even in adversity, and this ensures their survival, the survival of their families and the survival of their culture.

SAMPLE ANSWER

'Family, protest and identity are crucial for the survival of individuals.' How does *No Sugar* show this to be true?

Jack Davis' 1986 play *No Sugar* is a realist drama which examines the trials, tribulations and eventual survival of the Millimurra-Munday family through the Great Depression as they are forcibly removed from their homeland in Northam to the Moore River Native Settlement. The survival of their culture is dependent on the way that individuals shape their identity, and in this play Davis shows how family is the foundation on which identity can be maintained even in the most traumatic circumstances.

In Davis' play, Jimmy Munday survives and thrives as an individual because he has the support of his extended family. He finds his identity within his family and this security allows him to critically assess and comment on the motives behind government decisions such as the relocation of Indigenous people from the Government Well Aboriginal Reserve in Northam to Moore River. He says: 'Whole town knows why we're goin'. 'Coz *wetjalas* in this town don't want us 'ere.' Jimmy's identity and survival are built on outward protest but other members of his family find more subtle forms of protest.

Gran Munday is the matriarch and cornerstone of her family. She refuses to assimilate into a submissive Indigenous identity determined by white people. She looks after her family, providing them with a sense of cultural and practical knowledge. This is demonstrated when she insists on travelling with her family when moving to Moore River at the end of Act One, and when she delivers Mary's baby in Act Four. Gran is a survivor who passes on knowledge and language to her children and grandchildren, preserving her family and their identity in the face of extreme poverty and ongoing persecution.

In contrast, Billy Kimberley has lost his family and sense of identity. Being the last of his tribe and people, Billy Kimberley is caught between the Indigenous and non-Indigenous worlds and lacks a true sense of identity.

It is dramatically ironic that he is a 'successful' prototype of assimilation yet is rejected by both white and Indigenous societies. The children even mock him and call him a traitor or 'black crow'. Without family, ability to protest, or a clear identity, ultimately, not only will Billy not survive but his culture, traditions and family line will die with him also. It is this fate which also seems to await Mary Dargurru when we first meet her.

Mary is a young girl from the Kimberley region whose potential future can be paralleled to that of Billy who is from the same region. However, when she meets and falls in love with Joe Millimurra, she finds a new family in the Millimurras. She even finds the strength to stand up to the violent Neal: 'I don't care. You can belt me if you like, I'm not workin' in the hospital ... Go to hell!'. Mary not only finds her identity through family but has the potential at the end of the play to pass that identity on through her own family, as she begins a new life with Joe and their baby.

As a young man on the cusp of manhood, Joe Millimurra has a sense of his own destiny as shaped by his family and their connection to their culture and their homeland near Northam. He learns from his family that he must stand up for what he believes in and this shapes his identity and survival. At the end of the play, Joe, Mary and their newborn baby, Jimmy, leave with a sugar bag empty of 'white' rations (and metaphorically empty of the short-term sweet platitudes of white handouts, violence and condescension) but filled with much more valuable supplies; a homemade knife; and a sense of family, culture and identity that is hopefully enough to help them forge a new future in an old homeland.

Through Jimmy, Gran, Mary and Joe, Davis shows how individuals can survive numerous challenges to their dignity, health and freedom. These characters survive as a result of the integrity and resilience of their family, which gives them a strong sense of identity and the determination to resist white oppression. Although Jimmy dies, his legacy lives on through his nephew and his nephew's son. The survival of Billy, who has lost his family and identity, is fragile and lacking hope. In contrast, Joe and Mary leave for Northam full of hope for the next generation, symbolised in their baby son, Jimmy.

REFERENCES & READING

Text

Davis, Jack 2014, *No Sugar*, Currency Press, Strawberry Hills. First published in 1986.

Further reading

Casey, Mary Rose 2004, *Creating Frames: Contemporary Indigenous Theatre*, University of Queensland Press, Brisbane.

Cheeson, Keith 1988, *Jack Davis – A Biography*, Dent Press, Melbourne.

Davis, Jack 1984, *Kullark & The Dreamers*, Currency Press, Sydney.

Davis, Jack 1991, *A Boy's Life*, Magabala Books, Broome.

Eckersley, Mark 2012, *Australian Indigenous Drama*, Tasman Press, Altona.

Johnson, Colin 1988, 'Theatrical Fringe Benefits' in Ulli Beier and Colin Johnson, eds, *Long Water*, Aboriginal Arts Agency, Sydney, pp.1–17.

Sexton, Maureen 2000, 'Jack Davis 1917–2000', *Green Left Weekly*, 29 March, pp.25–6.

Shoemaker, Adam 1989, *Black Words White Page*, University of Queensland Press, Brisbane.

Shoemaker, Adam 1995, 'Jack Davis', in Philip Parsons and Victoria Chance, eds, *Companion to Theatre in Australia*, Currency Press, Strawberry Hills, Sydney.

Watego, Cliff 1990, *EN262 Black Australian Literature – Subject Reader*, University of Queensland, Brisbane.

Zalums, Elma & Stafford, Helen 1980, *A Bibliography of Western Australian Royal Commissions, Select Committees of Parliament and Boards of Enquiry, 1870–1979*, Blackwood Press, South Australia.